FLIGHT ROYAL
The Queen's Flight & Royal flying in five reigns

EIIR
THE QUEEN'S FLIGHT

FLIGHT ROYAL

The Queen's Flight & Royal flying in five reigns

Peter G. Cooksley

PSL Patrick Stephens, Cambridge

Frontispiece *Her Majesty pauses in the doorway of a Queen's Flight Andover machine at the end of the 1977 Jubilee Review of the RAF* (RAF News).

First published 1981

ISBN 0 85059 490 1

Text photoset in 10 on 10 pt Baskerville type by Manuset Limited, Baldock, Herts. Printed in Great Britain on 100 gsm Fineblade coated cartridge by Lowe & Brydone, Leeds, and bound by Norton-Bridge Bookbinders, Stotfold, Herts, for the publishers, Patrick Stephens Limited, Bar Hill, Cambridge, CB3 8EL, England

Contents

Typifying the association of the Royal Family with aviation in five reigns, the Royal Standard and the Royal Air Force Ensign fly together (MOD).

Preface

When the writing of a new book is begun, it is important, if it is to succeed, that the author approaches the subject, if not with humility, at least with a readiness to learn more. The planning stages of this work held several surprises, as might be expected from a subject about which a complete work has never before been attempted. Perhaps the chief among the impressions gained is the alarming quantity of work that is, and has long been, carried out annually by the Royal Family. The programme of responsibilities is such that the hardest-pressed of the Queen's subjects, who endure a 9 to 5 working day, would appear to be enjoying a permanent vacation by comparison.

Secondly, one begins to realise something of the reason for the massive popularity enjoyed by the late Duke of Windsor both as Prince of Wales and during his short reign, a popularity approached in our own changed age by Prince Charles, but expressed in a different way and for other reasons.

The final concern during the planning stages of this work was an anticipated shortage of material; not that this famine materialised, as will become clear when it is stated that the last problem was to present a balanced and representative history of both the Queen's Flight and its forerunners, together with the Royal Family's interest in aviation, when so much potential material had to be discarded in order to confine the book to its predetermined length.

Lastly I must state that any opinions that may seem to be submitted here are those of the writer alone and full responsibility is taken for them since they are not those of any other person or official in any position whatsoever.

Acknowledgements

Since a work of this type has never been attempted before, problems such as are associated with all pioneer efforts were encountered. However, these have been greatly eased by the ready and enthusiastic co-operation of several people to whom I am most grateful. Frequently their help consisted of recalling past events, the loan of documents and material or just pointing me in the right direction, but there was also the offer, made quite early in the planning stages, by the Queen's Press Secretary to look over the manuscript to confirm its accuracy. The full list of these co-operative gentlemen is as follows: The Right Honourable Lord Adeane of Stamfordham, PC, GCB, GCVO, MA; The Secretary of the Aircraft Owners and Pilots Association; Stanley Bruce; The Right Honourable Lord Charteris of Amisfield, PC, GCB, GCVO, OBE, QSO; Air Chief Marshal Sir Alec Coryton, KCB, KBE, MVO, DFC; The Director of Public Relations, Royal Australian Air Force; Bruce Robertson; The Secretary of the Royal Aero Club; Michael S. McA. Shea; Godfrey Talbot, MVO, OBE; Air Commodore Sir Archie L. Winskill, KCVO, CBE, DFC and Bar, AE, MRAeS.

I am also grateful to the editor of *Flight International* for permission to quote from that publication and reference sources have included past issues of *The Aeroplane, Flight* and *Popular Flying* among others.

The greater number of photographs in this book are Crown Copyright and I am grateful for permission to use them. The others have come either from my own files or the following persons and organisations to all of whom I am also indebted: British Airways; Norman W. Cruwys; The Fleet Air Arm Museum, Yeovilton, Somerset; *Flight International*; Hawker Siddeley; The Imperial War Museum, Lambeth; Photo News Limited; Planet News Limited; The Royal Australian Air Force; Bruce Robertson; Leonard D. Sorrell; *The Times*.

The remainder came either from the Canadian Public Archives, the Command Public Relations Offices of the RAF or the original collection of the former Westland Aircraft Company of Yeovil.

Peter G. Cooksley, London, 1980

King George V speaks to Captain Ira Jones at Château Le Nieppe near St Omer when visiting the 2nd Brigade, August 6 1918 (Imperial War Museum).

From Small Beginnings

'By viewing nature, nature's handmaid, art
Makes mighty things from small beginnings grow'
Thomas Dryden

'The King is dead, God save the King!' The seeming paradox of the Herald's cry had been heard at Temple Bar, throughout the City of London and had been echoed up and down the British Isles proclaiming the passing of the latest of a millennium of sovereigns of whom the more recent had held in their care the mightiest empire the world had ever known. Now the most illustrious of the civilised world had gathered on a day golden with May sunshine to escort to Windsor the last earthly remains of bluff, genial, human, King Edward VII.

'BB' Battery of the Royal Horse Artillery had been detailed to supply a gun, limber and eight-horse team for the coffin, while 'M' and 'Q' Batteries had each furnished under an officer a sub-section to form a composite unit for the London procession, to ride immediately in front of the Royal Navy and to the rear of the Household Cavalry which flanked further mounted troops.

Almost unnoticed among the marching men was a group who, could they but have known it, had before them an eventful and quite unique future. But they passed unremarked, except by a few of the better-informed in stiff, disciplined ranks along the sanded streets between houses, all spick and span with fresh paint and their frontages draped with the purple and black of mourning, the sombre colours contrasting with the brightness of the flags that waved at half-mast. These men were from the Corps of Royal Engineers and a small group had already seen service in the war against the Boers in South Africa and spent a protracted visit in Malta, six years before, in 1904.

With his outward-going nature and hopeful view of the future, rather than dwelling on the past, King Edward took a genuine interest in the many fresh advances in a wide spectrum of sciences which marked the new century. Perhaps the most immediately obvious of these was the royal interest in motor cars resulting in the fleet of Coventry Daimlers kept at Buckingham Palace, and the year before his death he had purchased a 65 hp four-cylinder Mercedes landaulette. This interest in matters mechanical was by no means confined to road transportation but extended to the flying machine, and during the very full final year of his life, the same one in which an obscure Frenchman was to render the focal point of the Empire an island no more, the King was to visit the Aero Show at Olympia at the end of March, an exhibition still giving balloons the same prominence as heavier-than-air machines.

King Edward's enthusiasm for the latter branch of aviation went considerably further than the 'keen' or alternatively 'lively interest' which writers have claimed until quite recently for all members of the Royal Family in everything and anything. His was a genuine desire to discover at first hand what direction the new sciences were taking. To this end he made use of one of his visits to Biarritz, a fashionable resort since the patronage of the Empress Eugenie, to drive over to Pau one Wednesday in mid-March 1909 where he had lunch, before going on to Pont Long where the Wright brothers had their flying ground. There had been plenty of time to prepare for the visit since the weather had been unsuitable for flying on both of the two previous days when the King had originally intended to come and, subsequently, a small welcoming party had been assembled in the form of the Mayor of Pau, Count Lambert, M. Tissandier, Wilbur and Orville Wright and their sister, Katherine. With Wilbur, the King went into the shed where the aeroplane was housed and the two spent some time in discussing the biplane. This proved to be an improved model with many refinements not present in the original 'Flyer' which had made the first portentous 12-second trip of a controlled and powered aeroplane at Kitty Hawk, a little less than six years earlier, and now boasted little additions such as improved rudders, seating for the pilot instead of the hip cradle—which also did duty as a means of control for the prone crewman—and also a second place so that a passenger might now be taken aloft.

While the photographers got through a number of plates, the two men talked as the light breeze, which indicated weather suitable for a flight, fluttered the American, British and French flags used for decoration before the biplane was taken from its shelter and, as the King looked on, started up and took to the air with Wilbur at the controls. Conscious of the critical knowledge that his visitor had shown, the pilot demonstrated the full capabilities of the machine before landing and helping his sister into the seat to his left. Rigged for take-off once more the frail aeroplane was shot into the air and Wilbur now took it to a height, then remarked as being 'considerable', before making a spectacular shallow dive in order to fly past the King at very low altitude. This done, the pilot climbed again and then set off towards Pau itself, being out of sight for more than five minutes.

Back home in Britain, King Edward VII redoubled his efforts to see that departments of his Government were aware of the implications of the new science, but there were darkening clouds on the aviation horizon which he realised could spoil all that had gone before. These took the form of a growing rivalry between the various bodies which had appeared with a view to controlling aviation. Aware that such a state of affairs could result in deepening divisions, as the struggle for seniority became more acute, the King took the same step as he had with the Automobile Club in 1907 and granted the title 'Royal' to the Aero Club in 1910, thus giving authority to the organisation which had existed as an offspring of the motoring body since October 1901, having been preceded by the Balloon Society.

With the reign of King Edward's successor, his eldest surviving son George V, only two weeks old, some of the effort of the late monarch in the governmental field seemed to bear fruit when an impressive group of British representatives attended the International Conference on Aerial Navigation in Paris, consisting of delegates from the Admiralty, the Army Council and the Secretary of State for the Home Department, and numbering among them such names scheduled to pass into aviation history as that of Captain Murray Sueter RN.

It is no secret that the new King, surprisingly for a younger man, had, on a personal level, no particular liking for aviation. Nevertheless, in accordance with his stated policy as one who should 'advise, observe and encourage', he did his duty and continued to give the same backing to the art of flying that his father had done, despite the fact that his heart and training marked him out as a Naval officer, a state of affairs which was to have an unexpected influence on the advance of aeronautics in a short space of time.

However, by the summer of 1910, it was becoming widely accepted that flying had distinct military possibilities. The first Army manoeuvres of the new reign saw the use of private aeroplanes, a fact which, with the benefit of hindsight, the more superstitious were to remember in conjunction with the appearance of Halley's Comet the same year, and remark on the belief held since 1066, when Harold Gowinson had died at the hands of William the Norman's men at Senlac, that a great evil was to smite the land when the fiery harbinger was seen. An easily-understood attitude in the days to come when aerial attack was to destroy for ever the myth of an Englishman's home being an inviolate castle.

Coronation year—1911—was to be marked in the British aviation world by a fresh departure with the formation of the new Air Battalion of the Royal Engineers, when, on February 28, an Army Order was promulgated announcing the formation to take effect from the following April 1. This Battalion was to consist of two companies, one concentrating on the use of aeroplanes, while the other specialised in airships. The smallness of the new unit, which had its Headquarters at South Farnborough, was emphasised by the total establishment for only 14 officers and 176 non-commissioned men.

The late spring and early summer of the following year was to see a great upsurge of aviation support and development. The first of these was to take place during May at the Naval Review when various military seaplanes flew over the Royal Yacht, the *Victoria and Albert,* while one set down on the sea and taxied sufficiently close to the Royal vessel for a letter to be handed aboard addressed to the King. At the same Review it was remarked that HMS *Hibernia* (one of the King Edward Class Pre-Dreadnoughts known as the 'Wobbly Eight' which had been completed between 1904-6 at a cost of some £1,450,000 each) was equipped with a launching platform for a pair of 'Hydro-aeroplanes' as they were termed at the time, and it was one of these Short biplanes that Commander Samson RN used to make a pioneer fly-off from this vessel; the first from a moving ship, at the self-same Royal Review of the Fleet. Perhaps it was due to the unreliable nature of the motors of the time that these S38 machines boasted flotation bags in addition to wheels.

Royal aviation connections continued that year when, during the next month, Sir Sidney Greville presented Gustav Hamel to the King. Hamel had just completed an exhibition of airmanship in a newly-acquired two-seat Blériot monoplane fitted with a 70 hp motor, and in which Captain Mark Kerr RN flew as a passenger. Ten minutes after his take-off from Hendon, Hamel arrived at about 4.45 pm, flying at some 3,000 feet over the polo fields of the Ranelagh Club. About an hour and a quarter later the two men once more took-off and gave an aerobatic display for 15 minutes after the finals of the Aldershot Day competition were over and the field cleared. Having landed the Blériot, with the prominent number '3' on the rudder immediately in front of the pavilion occupied by King George and Queen Mary, who were accompanied by Mary, later the Princess Royal, the two aviators removed their flying overalls to reveal neatly-cut lounge suits and donned straw boaters before being conducted to the royal presence.

The year 1912 was also rich in other aviation events emanating from the Royal Family, one being when the Keeper of the King's Privy Purse, Sir William Carington, despatched, on the King's behalf, a letter to the Chairman of the Royal Aero Club stating that His Majesty had decided to honour that organisation with his Patronage. No doubt the few who noticed this fact recorded obscurely at the bottom of a column in their breakfast-time newspapers mentally equated it with another event that had taken place five weeks previously. This was the adoption of the proposals of a sub-committee of the Committee of Imperial Defence which had advocated the establishment of a single Flying Corps consisting of Naval and Military Wings plus a Central Flying School. But the step taken when George V put his signature to the Royal Warrant on April 13 was a very important one, for it created, exactly one month later, the Royal Flying Corps that one day was to grow into the RAF and which, within six years, was to attain a strength of 293,532 officers and men.

The war-clouds had scarcely begun to gather on the political horizons of Europe when in May 1913 King George paid a visit to Aldershot and inspected some of the rather motley collection of types flown by the Royal Flying Corps while, later that same month, their Majesties were once more made aware of the many possibilities of the aeroplane when the Royal yacht *Victoria and Albert* was provided with an escort from a Short machine, piloted by Sub-Lieutenant J.T. Babington RN, during its journey in connection with the visit of the King and Queen to Berlin. In order to provide this, the H1 aeroplane took off from the then-new Naval air station on the Isle of Grain, with its twin facilities for sea and landplanes, and followed the Royal Vessel to a point some 18 miles from Margate before circling and returning to base.

The following year, George V paid his usual visit to the Aero Show at Olympia, as he had attended on the opening day in 1913, but, during the same month, both he and Queen Mary were able to have a more personal view of the developing aeroplane on their own doorstep, as it were, when Gustav Hamel flew to Windsor from Hendon early in February. Hamel was now flying a Morane Saulnier machine fitted with an 80 hp motor. He arrived over the Long Walk at about 12.45 pm to find that his coming was expected by more than the Royal Family for, despite the day being a working Thursday, a large crowd had gathered to watch the novel spectacle of a flying machine visiting their king. The display which the pilot gave was one of his best and took up some ten minutes before the machine was brought down to a smooth landing on the East Terrace of the castle. Once out of the cockpit Hamel was presented again to the King and Queen who later looked the machine over and noticed the contrast with the Blériot they had inspected on the previous occasion at Ranelagh. In this they were supported by Princess Mary again, as well as Prince Henry, later Duke of Gloucester, and nine-year-old Prince John.

After lunch at Windsor Castle, Hamel once more took-off and gave a further demonstration of some half hour's duration before making off towards Hendon again. A further visit took place on the following Monday and, once again, the flyer's arrival was anticipated by a substantial crowd when he made his appearance just after mid-day and landed once more on the East Lawn, the stretch of grass which was to figure so significantly in the early days of the King's Flight almost three decades later. On this occasion Hamel was welcomed on landing by the King and Queen as before in company with Prince John and his aunt, Princess Maud. After the usual exchanges, Gustav Hamel took off and, during a 17-minute exhibition, executed no less than 14 loops. Having then landed for lunch, he gave a further display of aerobatics before turning for Hendon.

As the spring of 1914 ripened into early summer, King George paid a visit in May to the Aircraft Park at Farnborough, Hampshire, and became the subject of a pair of early experiments. On leaving the tent where he had been received, the King noticed two RFC machines circling overhead. One of these was equipped with radio and the other carried a camera. Before even he had mounted his charger the first aircraft had sent a wireless message that King George was on his way so that the reception party which included the Director General of Military Aeronautics, Brigadier-General Sir David Henderson, and Lieutenant-Colonel Sir

Frederick Sykes might be ready. Both of these officers were to serve their King and Country well in the coming holocaust, the former commanding Squadrons 2, 3, 4 and 5 when they left Dover's Swingate Downs to begin the fight in France the following August, while the other was to act as his Chief Staff Officer.

Drawn up on the far side of the field were 27 machines with the pilots and mechanics paraded in front. While this inspection was going on, the photographic experts were hard at work and, only 14 minutes after the machine with the camera had landed, prints were ready for the King showing himself riding across the field. But the demonstration of modern expertise was not yet over for, soon after, there took place an exhibition of communication with an aeroplane in flight by wireless telegraphy by means of a Morse transmitter on the ground. A notable achievement, for the first British aircraft had been fitted with radio only two years before, making ground to air transmission possible and, during 1914, the first exchange of wireless communication between aircraft in flight was to take place over a range of ten miles.

However, although all this seemed very wonderful, the King had come to accept that aeroplanes, although noisy, smelly things, were a necessary part of his armed forces. This had been borne out on the occasion of his official birthday celebrations on Laffan's Plain in June of the previous year when, contained in an area of perhaps a square mile, five Brigades had paraded for inspection and marched past to the accompaniment of a salute of 21 guns from the far side of the canal.

This had included a taxi-past of 13 aeroplanes, made up of six Maurice Farmans, two Henry Farmans, four BE biplanes of various types including the BE3 and, it is fairly certain to assume, the original BE1, known as the 'Army Silent Aeroplane' from the silencers fitted to the exhausts. The single representative of the Blériot Monoplane was number 221, a Model XI series II. But this, the first Royal inspection of the RFC, was probably marked for most of the spectators by the presence of the two Army airships, *Gamma,* the first non-rigid to be fitted with swivel propellers for improved landing and take-off control, and *Beta*, also dating in its latest form from 1912, when it was fitted with a larger engine of 35 hp.

After the marching men who had flanked the aeroplanes made their way past the saluting base and dispersed, the machines took-off for a final fly-past. There followed an incident that had an almost modern ring about it and may well be the first recorded case of bird hazard from a flock, although it post-dated the well-known encounters with eagles that Gilbert and Vedrines experienced during the Paris to Madrid Air Race in May 1911. On this later occasion the spectators were treated to the sight of 13 aircraft making their way in one direction while a great gathering of crows, numbering many thousands, seemed bent on a collision course at the same altitude and from exactly the opposite direction. When their field of view became obscured by the birds, the pilots changed course to each side and over and under the flock, with one exception in the form of one of the Maurice Farmans which kept straight on, evidently in an attempt to see whose nerve would break first. Strangely it was the pilot's that finally admitted defeat when he flung his machine into a left hand bank and dived clear at the last minute, leaving the crows to go on their way in an unbroken and seemingly inexorable cloud.

On July 1 1914 the provisions of the Royal Warrant, to which Georve V had put his signature a little earlier, took effect and there was thus created from the former Naval Wing of the RFC, the Royal Naval Air Service. But, whatever their title, military flyers were, in little over a month, to receive their baptism of fire for, three days before the new Service came into being, Gavrilo Princip, a sickly 19-year-old member of the amateurish Black Hand Gang of political fanatics, had committed double murder at Sarajevo, the capital of Bosnia.

With his strong sense of Royal duty, King George was among the first of the monarchs of the warring nations to visit his men in the field and more than one 'Tommy' remarked on the sight of his king taking an alfresco meal from the back of a lorry doing duty as a table in the open air, but the visit to France of 1915 to units, including those of the Royal Flying Corps, was to alter the course of the remainder of his life.

Troubled at the increasing lack of confidence that the Generals freely admitted to for the irascible Sir John French, the Commander in Chief since the dreadful retreat from Mons, the King had spent much time in serious conversation with General Robertson on the suitability of appointing Sir Douglas Haig, then in command of the First Army instead of French. He was scheduled to follow these talks on the next day, Thursday, October 28, with a visit to Sir Douglas' command at Labuissière. This done, he then drove to Hesdigneul to inspect part of the 1st Wing of the Royal Flying Corps which occupied the curious L-shaped aerodrome there. The King made a short speech after the inspection, congratulating the men on the good work they were doing. He then turned to ride down the lines of men drawn up beside the main Bethune to Bruay road, mounted on a chestnut mare, lent for the occasion by Sir Douglas Haig. When he was about mid-way between the Bessonneau Hangar and the farmhouse on the south side someone called for a cheer. At the sudden outburst of noise the horse reared up, and one of the few surviving witnesses to the incident remembers vividly the small detail, as one does on such occasions, of the immaculate white picket rope flashing between the pawing front hooves in the moment before the horse's hind ones slipped in the mud to send it over backwards pinning His Majesty underneath. This was Percy Butcher, an engine fitter of No 2 Squadron, one of the group of NCOs who helped push the horse off the King and carry him to his car, which gave him an agonising journey to the house, just outside Aire, which did duty as a hospital since his injuries included a double fracture of the pelvis.

Here the King lay for the next three days and, during this time, all who knew what had happened were sworn to secrecy to prevent the news leaking out to the Germans, and several squadrons, including Numbers 2 and 3, kept a constant patrol over the vicinity. It is not without interest to note that, among the airmen who did this, were Lieutenant Johnson in a two-seat Morane with an Air Mechanic, James McCudden, in the rear seat who policed the area on at least one occasion for a space of three hours.

On November 1 His Majesty was pronounced well enough to be moved by train to Boulogne and it was during this journey that he bestowed the Victoria Cross, from his bed, on Lance-Sergeant Oliver Brooks of the Coldstream Guards, before making the exhausting journey across the Channel in the *Anglia* and then to Buckingham Palace where it was some four weeks before he could begin to walk short distances again, and then only with the aid of two sticks. There were those near to the King who claimed that his recovery was never really complete.

Following his return to his duties, George V made several further visits to the Western Front and, at each of these, he was protected by constant air patrols, a precedent established during the first trip to France and the British and Belgian sectors in Flanders in December 1914 when he had been shown a captured German machine. So it is not at all surprising that, in the middle of April 1917, it was announced that the King had assumed the title of Colonel-in-Chief of the Royal Flying Corps and, during the following July, His Majesty was accompanied to France by Queen Mary. Several RNAS units were visited, as well as those of the RFC, although the strain on his constitution was now becoming obvious, a fact remarked on by his mother as well as the United States Ambassador.

One of the most arduous of these royal tours was that during August 1918 which included visits to the squadrons of the First Brigade at Izel-le-Hameau and of the Second Brigade at Château Le Nieppe near St Omer. At the former, which took place on August 8, No 203 was among the

King George V visiting Izel-le-Hameau in August 1918, the Headquarters of the 1st Brigade. Raymond Collishaw may be noted, just behind the King, by his Naval cap.

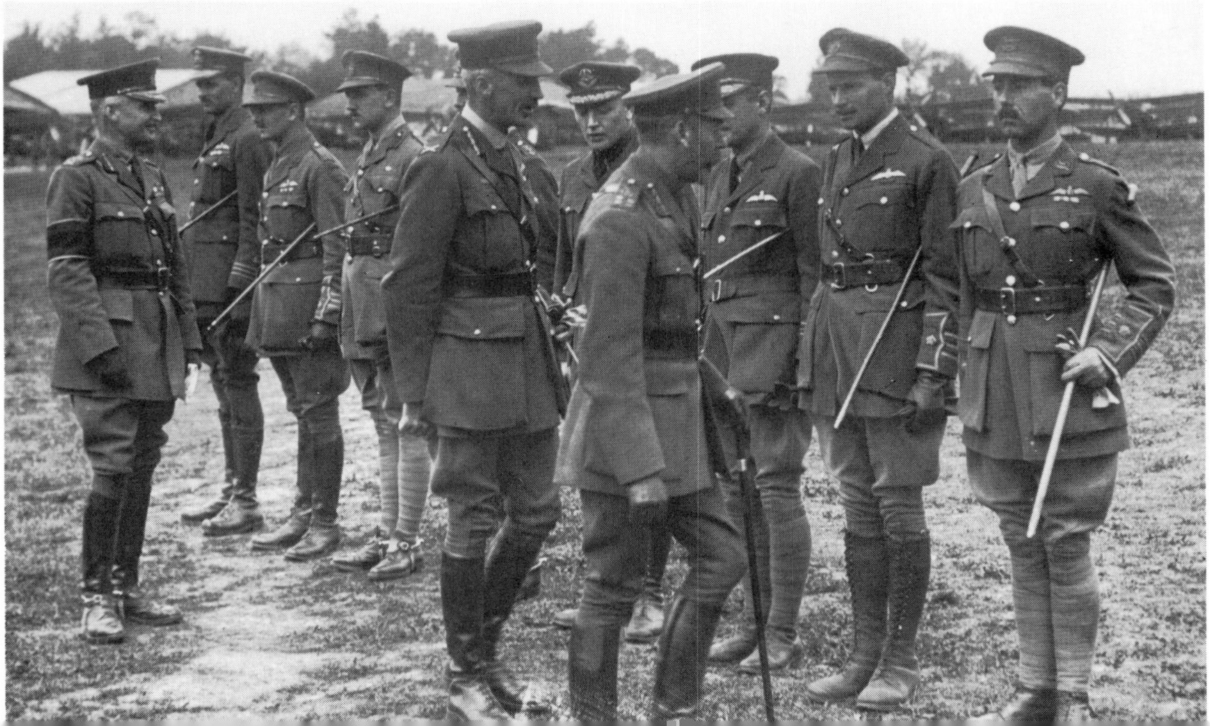

squadrons inspected; this had its Sopwith Camels lined up in front of the hangars with each Flight Commander at attention beside his machine. His Majesty walked slowly along the line, pausing to speak to many of the officers, in the company of Major Raymond Collishaw, the Commanding Officer, who was to meet the King again during the years to come. The King's escort, both on this occasion and during the earlier introduction to the commanders, consisted of Brigadier General Pitcher, Brigade Commander, and General Sir Henry Horne, in charge of the British First Army, who was later to depart in the same car with the King which was 'seen off' by a loudly barking Peter, the brindle bulldog belonging to 203.

The Royal visit to the air units of the Second Brigade had taken place two days previously, in company with General Plumer, Brigadier General Webb-Bowen and Sir Henry Horne again. Among the pilots paraded were Captain J. Ira T. ('Taffy') Jones who was to record the event in his diary as 'The greatest day in my life'. Others included Captain S. Carlin, who could only claim 11 victories to Jones' 40 and could be easily picked out by the fact that he wore 'slacks' instead of the regulation breeches, since he had a wooden leg that had earned him the name of 'Timbertoes' in No 74 Squadron. But possibly one of the most interesting officers whom the King met was Captain E. Roxburgh-Smith, victor in 16 aerial combats. At over 30 years of age he was older than the average scout pilot, and was married with children, having given up a career as a bank clerk in Bromley, Kent, to enlist in the Royal Flying Corps to eventually become the pilot of one of No 92 Squadron RAF's SE5as.

It had been a long, hard tour of duty for George V, stretching back to July 5 1917 when he had inspected the squadrons at Bray Dunes. These included No 3 RNAS appearing for the last time as a Naval squadron for, by April the next year, it was part of something entirely new, a separate Air Force of which the King (as he remarked in a telegram marking the occasion to Lord Rothermere, Secretary of State for the new Service) was General-in-chief, and it was in this new capacity that the wearisome tour of inspection had been cheerfully undertaken in the final summer months of 1918.

His Majesty was not the only member of the Royal Family to encourage the new arm, however, for during that same August there had taken place an interesting little ceremony in connection with the increasing public interest in 'Presentation' machines, bearing the name of the donor. The aircraft in question was a Sopwith F1 Camel, subscribed for by the not-yet 'Royal' Army Service Corps and at Isleworth it was named by Princess Patricia, daughter of Arthur, Duke of Connaught, who was also present, a brother of King Edward VII. The machine, having been blessed by Bishop Taylor-Smith, Chaplain-General to the Forces, was then flown off with Lieutenant H.C. Sanderson at the controls of 'Osterley No 1', after he had been presented with a silver cigarette box to mark the occasion, in the presence of General Branker, who had only just returned from the United States.

In an atmosphere such as this with almost every member of the Royal Family interested in varying degrees in the art and science of aviation, four young men were growing up in the Royal household with the normal keen intelligence of youth and consequent thirst to widen their knowledge of all

Cadets of the Hastings officer training school march past King George V near West Marina Gardens, St Leonards-on-Sea, Sussex, about 1918 (Crown Copyright).

things new; the four surviving sons of King George V. The eldest of these was Edward, Prince of Wales, who already held a commission in the Army, while the next was Albert, traditionally bearing the title Duke of York, as the King's second son, and it was these two young princes who were to lay the foundations of that which is to-day known as the Queen's Flight.

There were two sets of circumstances that brought this about, the earlier taking place in 1918 on the Italian Front. This sector was being visited by Prince Edward during the summer and, while at Villaverla, he was invited to fly with Captain W.G. Barker of No 139 Squadron as a passenger in a Bristol F2B Fighter. The actual machine used for this historic occasion was DF8063 'D' although it seems likely that more than one trip was taken if the well-known photograph of the Prince and the Captain in a Biff marked 'S' is anything to go by. With his tour of duty completed, the two men parted, the Prince returned to England while Barker, now a Major, was posted to No 201 Squadron on the Western Front, largely at his own insistence since it was felt that this Canadian officer should in fact take a rest. Now with a single-seat unit flying Bentley Camels, apart from his personal evaluation model of a Sopwith Snipe, there was little time in the busy skies of the Beugnatre sector, where he was supposed to be taking a 'refresher' during October, to recall that he had carried the

Above *The Prince of Wales flies in a Bristol Fighter of No 139 Squadron in Italy.* **Below** *Edward, Prince of Wales, with Captain Barker, VC, in a Bristol F2B* (Imperial War Museum).

Heir Apparent over enemy lines on what was, in fact, Prince Edward's second air experience, for his first flight had been a little-recorded trip during 1916, before the Somme Battle.

On October 27 Barker was on his way to Hounslow for leave when he decided to add an enemy two-seater to his score, and it was while watching the final moments of this that the Snipe was set upon by several Fokkers; three went down quite quickly but not before first the Canadian's right thigh, then his left leg, and finally his left elbow, were all torn open by bullets. The pilot was semi-conscious from loss of blood when another bullet destroyed the ignition system and he retained just enough comprehension to crash-land the machine inside the Allied lines. Strangely this spectacular action was to have repercussions in unexpected places in the fullness of time but, during almost the same period, the Prince of Wales was flying with Major Greig in a Handley Page 0/400. Following the signing of the Armistice in April, the Prince flew in a similar type over London, with several passengers, piloted by Lieutenant Carruthers, as well as in an American Expeditionary Force machine over the Rhineland with Brigadier General William (Billy) L. Mitchell, the fiery believer in all-out air power who had distinguished himself in the struggle for the St Mihiel salient, at the controls.

Meanwhile, Prince Edward's younger brother, Prince Albert, was faced with something of a dilemma. As a Naval officer he had seen action in HMS *Collingwood* during the Battle of Jutland but, about three months later, he had to be transferred to shore duties due to a recurring duodenal ulcer. This was finally operated on following his last period at sea in HMS *Malaya*.

Recovering from this while the war was still on meant that he could not appear to be idle and, since he could no longer be expected to endure the rigours of life in the Royal Navy, the Duke of York therefore joined the Royal Naval Air Service, since he had privately shown a genuine interest and sympathy for the efforts of Trenchard. The Prince therefore found himself serving for just over eight months at HMS *Daedalus,* otherwise the bleak, hutted training establishment at Cranwell in Lincolnshire. Here, he had charge of the boys' squadron and found some difficulty in understanding the new relaxed atmosphere which contrasted with the long-established attitudes of punctiliousness he had grown used to in the Royal Navy. However, the care for over 2,000 boys fully occupied his time and the problems of understanding them in no way reflected his genuine belief in the future of the new Air Force.

Having served for a few weeks on the staff at Nancy to widen his experience, the Duke of York returned to England early in 1919 after firmly deciding to learn to fly, and he was consequently attached to the staff in London and sent to the Government Aerodrome, Waddon, Surrey, later Croydon Airport, to learn flying.

At a dinner in later years the Prince was to describe himself as 'a very moderate pilot'. His hearers took this to be modesty but in fact it was more; a truthful statement of fact for, surprisingly for a good horseman, he was not completely at home in the air, a state of affairs he was never able to remedy with practice, due to the unending calls on his time which are the lot of princes.

His training had begun under Captain Alec Coryton, a young officer who was exactly the same age as the Duke, during February 1919, at which time there were strange reports that a specially-built Avro 504 was being prepared at Hamble for royal use at St Andrée, near Boulogne. They were correct in the naming of the type of aircraft but in little else,

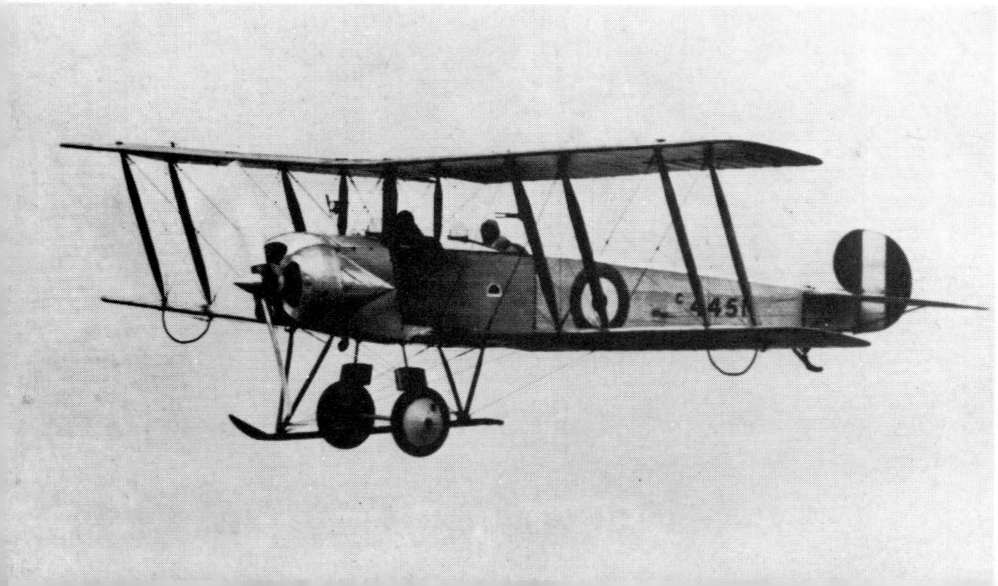

Prince Albert with his instructor lands at Waddon (Croydon) Aerodrome in an Avro 504J. They were approaching across Coldharbour Lane, later Purley Way (Crown Copyright).

for Avro 504J, C4451, was neither new nor special but the survivor of two crashes, a fact which later caused some concern at the Air Ministry. Captain Coryton was ordered to obtain a new machine, albeit much too late, for the veteran machine was to be used for another Prince about the following May!

Always a closely-knit group, the Royal Family seemed to find an answer to Prince Albert's training problems when he was joined by his elder brother, Prince Edward. His instructors, at first Major Bird who was later posted away, and later Captain Stanley Vincent, found him a natural pilot who was soon asking for the experience of aerobatics and, following a cross-wind take-off when the wing fender touched the ground, Captain Vincent was reproved by an equerry, who knew nothing of flying, for behaving dangerously! Despite his enjoyment of flight the Prince of Wales was doing no more than lending some moral support to his brother, who was determined to gain his 'wings' and, as events later evolved, this was all to the good.

Shortly after his experience over London which he shared with Lady Joan Mulholland, Lord Claud Hamilton and Mark Kerr of the Ranelagh Club demonstration, now an Admiral, Prince Edward once more happened to meet Major Barker, newly invested Victoria Cross holder and recovering from his wounds received in the fight of October 1918. Those to his legs had largely healed as it was now May of the following year, but he still had only limited use of his arm. He invited the Prince for a flight over the weekend and, on the day following the party, the two men met again at Hounslow and were watched by T.O.M. Sopwith as they prepared to go aloft in the prototype Sopwith Dove, a two-seat derivative of the wartime Pup. The following flight was significant for the number of aerobatics carried out, despite the fact that Barker had to hook his wounded arm round the throttle in order to operate it.

All this was reported in some of the daily papers on the next day with such headlines as that in the *Daily Mirror* which announced that the 'Prince of Wales stunts with one-armed VC!' This error of fact was echoed in the next issue of *Flight* magazine (which should have known better) which stated that Barker had 'lost one arm as a result of his wonderful war work'.

There is naturally no question that King George was better informed than the press in these matters but his first knowledge of the incident had come from these columns, so that he immediately sent for his eldest son. It has often been related since that His Majesty immediately forbade the Prince to fly again since the man with his arm in a sling had not been the official instructor, but this hardly seems correct for at almost the same time Winston Churchill, who had no aptitude for flying, had nearly suffered a fatal crash at Croydon, and it was the combination of these two events which caused the King, during what must surely have been a stern interview, to counsel his son not to fly again.

Prince Albert, however, continued his course and all went well for a time as he steadily built up his air experience, which included, at an earlier period, not only that gained in a Handley Page bomber about a year before at Cranwell, but also a flight in a two-seat Sopwith Camel at the same station. As during the last months of the war, so with the first period of peace, the sight of the Duke of York assisting his father with his official duties, as well as performing his own public functions in the uniform of an RAF Lieutenant, was becoming increasingly commonplace. As witness the time when he laid the foundation stone of a new merchantile school at Poole, Dorset in May, visited the Great International Sports Carnival at Stamford Bridge, or was seen at

The Sopwith Dove prototype in which the Prince of Wales flew with Major Barker, VC.

T.O.M. Sopwith, the Prince of Wales and Major Barker beside the Dove in which the latter pair are about to fly. Note that Barker is adjusting the sling for his arm (Canadian Public Archives).

The Prince of Wales in the rear cockpit of the Sopwith Dove with Major W.G. Barker, VC, forward.

The Duke of York with his instructor beside an Avro 504K (Crown Copyright).

Bisley when he presented the King's Prize and at the annual inspection of the Foundling Hospital in June. However, it was always without a pilot's brevet above his medal ribbons that he appeared, but this was soon to be righted. But at this point, a problem presented itself in the form of the necessary medical examination for, although he was certainly fit enough to fly, the medical board was reluctant to permit him to fly alone in the light of his past history, so that a simple compromise had to be sought.

This resulted in his final qualifying flight in July taking the form of a trip, not solo as is usual but with his instructor; 'Prince Albert never flew solo for his tests etc', Captain (now Air Chief Marshal Sir Alec) Coryton was to recall for the author, 'I flew in the front seat and he in the back'. By August 1919 when the Prince presented the prizes at the Queen's Club, West London, sports meeting he was now seen to be a qualified pilot and, shortly after, he was gazetted a Squadron Leader. By the time of the all-important flight, a fresh machine had at last been obtained, this time an Avro 504K built by the parent company; H2314 fitted with a Monosoupape motor, officially on the strength of No 24 Squadron. In after years two interesting, if minor, events were to result from this.

The first of these had its beginning during the same summer when the Government Aerodrome at Croydon was closed down and the aircraft and instructors transferred to nearby Kenley where the Avro machine continued to be used for other pupils over the following 12 months. In the autumn of 1920 Alec Coryton was posted to Cranwell and, before his departure, thought he would like to retain the control column from the machine as a souvenir of its royal associations, so this was removed from H2314 and replaced with one from a crashed Avro.

It remained in the family for the next 28 years until the death of Alec Coryton's father-in-law in whose home it had been, when everything was sold, and at this point it was thought that Prince Albert, now His Majesty King George VI, might like to have the item. In about 1948 it was offered to the King via Louis Greig, the naval surgeon who had been among the King's friends since before their service days in 1917 aboard HMS *Malaya.* The offer was accepted and Air Commodore Coryton, now commanding No 11 Group, Fighter Command, set about the problem of having the stick suitably mounted. In this he consulted the Goldsmiths and Silversmiths Company which devised two; one with the column mounted vertically, more representative of the position in the machine, the other displaying it on a plinth horizontally. The former was chosen by the King who also slightly revised the suggested inscription and requested that this be attached to the top of the display mounting instead of the side as had originally been intended. Some short time later, when the work had been carried out, the donor was personally summoned to Buckingham Palace to present the historic item to His Majesty and it remains in the Royal collection to-day bearing a small silver plaque with the following words: 'The control column used by King George VI in Avro aeroplane No H2314, when as HRH The Prince Albert he went through his flying training course at Croydon, and gained his Wings in July, 1919. Lt W.A. Coryton, RAF was his instructor'.

More public was the other occurrence in connection with the early days of the first pilot-king, taking place as it did at the original post-war RAF Display held at Farnborough, Hants, early in July 1950. Several early machines were displayed among the modern aircraft, to a crowd of over 70,000 and to a Royal party led by George VI and Queen Elizabeth and including Princess Margaret, Marshal of the Royal Air Force Sir John and Lady Slessor, Air Chief Marshal the Honourable Sir Ralph Cochrane and the Air Minister, Mr Arthur Henderson. In weather forecast to be poor, but in fact pleasant and bright, a surviving Avro 504 was displayed. While the King watched, Group Captain L.S. Snaith, AFC, Commandant of the Empire Test Pilots' School, on his first flight in the type since 1927, excepting the dress rehearsal on July 5, made what was later described as a 'dicey-looking take-off' and put the machine through its paces. It was commonly declared that this item had been included in the programme for the monarch's pleasure and was even said to have been finished to represent the aircraft in which he took his wings. Perhaps this was so, but it was strangely numbered H2311.

Watching it, the King's mind must have gone back to another day in July, exactly 30 years before when he had visited the RAF Pageant, then usually described as the Tournament, in the company of his younger brother, Prince Henry, Duke of Gloucester, and attended by the GOC London District, General G.D. Jeffreys, while almost exactly a month previously, on June 9, his father had been present at the opening of the Olympia Aero Exhibition.

The Duke of York was now a Squadron Leader and his promotion was to be seen on occasions such as when he visited the RAF College at Cranwell, presenting new Colours to the 20th Battalion of the London Regiment, the Empire Day celebrations in Hyde Park and the opening of the new Marylebone Town Hall. And, within the year, he was a Wing Commander visiting industrial Dartford, and bestowing the Distinguished Flying Cross on King

An Avro 504K restored and marked H2311 to represent the type in which George VI trained. This was shown to him at the Farnborough RAF display in July 1950 (N.W. Cruwys).

Albert of the Belgians. Within a space of time too, his father, George V, was to only once perform his public duties in the uniform of a Marshal of the Royal Air Force and he also wore a pilot's Wings as his Royal Prerogative, although he never flew as did his sons.

These changes were symptomatic of a new and different world that was appearing out of the chaos of the First World War, not only in the United Kingdom, but in Europe and throughout the world; these were to combine with another revolution that was taking place quietly and without undue note at the little RAF aerodrome established on common land as No 7 Aircraft Acceptance Park during the summer of 1917, at Kenley, Surrey. After the end of hostilities this became the base of No 1 (Communications) Squadron and, while the Peace Conference was meeting in the Hall of Mirrors at the Palace of Versailles, a regular air service was flown with DH4As and Handley Page 0/400s between Kenley and Paris. At first these journeys during 1919 and 1920 might seem small and of little consequence, but in fact they were to have far-reaching results and bring about a further step in the slow evolution of a Royal Flight, for the conveyance of these delegates, and communications was to establish a new precedence, namely the use of aircraft for VIP purposes.

Peace is Come

'Peace is come and wars are over
Welcome you and welcome all'
Alfred Edward Housman

When the last round of ammunition had been fired on the Western Front and the cheers of the last merry-maker had died away, there were many who believed that life would now resume the pace of the days before the carnage had descended on the world, but they were wrong for it was not a man and his wife who had been shot dead in Bosnia but a generation and an age.

One of the main reasons why the old world, for better or worse, had gone for ever was because the increased pace of invention during the years of hate had given men so much that was new that a whole industry swiftly arose to beat, as soon as possible, the proverbial swords into ploughshares. Foremost among these was the flying machine and it seemed not seven years but an age away that an ingenuous delight had greeted such strides along the path of progress as that in 1911 when 100,000 letters and cards had been flown in eight trips from Hendon to Windsor by the pilots of the Blériot and Grahame-White Schools operating the famous first UK aerial post. Among the mail had been those cards celebrating the Coronation addressed 'To His Majesty The King, Windsor Castle'.

That same year had seen a flight to Windsor under very different conditions since it was carried out one cold, foggy February morning when the water froze in the radiator pipes as it was being filled. Even so, since his King had expressed a desire to see the machine, the pilot decided he must make the attempt and arrived to find Windsor bathed in sunlight. Making a temporary landing on Datchet golf links in order to inspect the Royal 'landing strip' after lunch, he finally arrived on the East Lawn on a bright winter afternoon. Here he was greeted by Sir Charles Cust of the Royal Household who, earlier in the day, had assisted him in picking out a suitable spot, and now introduced him to George V. The formalities over, the King, in the company of three of his sons, looked the Howard Wright biplane over and, as is the way of those things on occasions when all is wanted to appear perfect, one of the first things on which the royal eye alighted was the slow trickle of water from the radiator leak! The 'intrepid airman' who had to explain the problems of the morning to the King was named T.O.M. Sopwith and now, in the first months of the new peace after the 'war to end wars' his name was almost a household word as the head of a vast aircraft manufacturing company now turning its attention to the possible application of the aeroplane for new uses.

'Tommy' Sopwith was not alone in this for the same idea was in the minds of many and foremost among these supporters of commercial aviation was the Press. An occasion arose quite quickly when it became possible to use the aeroplane to speed communications when King George V and Queen Mary were to open the Northern Ireland Parliament in Belfast. This excited great comment at the time when photographs of the event were found in the next morning's newspapers, not only in London but also the Midlands and Scotland, but greatest acclaim of all was reserved for the Pathé film company who made it possible for cinema-goers in the capital to see the royal ceremonies in Ireland that same June evening in 1921.

The previous year had been marked by the announcement that King George V had once more given his Royal patronage to the Aero Exhibition scheduled to open at Olympia on June 9, and the following month, Prince Henry, in company with the GOC London District, General G.D. Jeffreys, had paid a visit to the RAF Pageant held in aid of the Memorial Fund on Saturday, July 3, the very first of what was to become later known as the RAF Display. This was the beginning of what was to become a Hendon tradition lasting until 1937. The aircraft demonstrated on that pioneer day, organised in reality to restore flagging Service self-esteem in the face of the cuts in government spending of that time, included ex-war types such as the Sopwith Snipe, Bristol Fighters, Avro 504s and even an airworthy Fokker D VII, one of the few flyable specimens left from the hundreds with which Germany had ended the war. But the visit by the Prince was in no way carried out in a spirit of grudging duty for, in common with many of the other young men of his day, he was doing no more than taking a closer look at a subject that interested him.

Perhaps there was something of the thought of supporting this attitude of mind behind the King's decision to present a trophy, to be known as the King's Cup, for annual award to the winner of an aerial circuit of Great Britain, the first such event to take place on Friday, September 8 of that same year, 1922, and so replace the London Air Derby as the high spot of the aviation year.

The course was to total some 850 miles divided into two sections, Waddon, Birmingham, Newcastle to Glasgow and Glasgow, Manchester, Bristol to Waddon—the latter being that same station in Surrey where two of the Royal brothers had gained some air experience and which was later to be better remembered as Croydon Aerodrome, the pre-1939 London Airport.

Starting time from both ends of the course was set for 9 am and the total number of entrants was 22, for the most part flying ex-wartime machines or derivatives converted for passenger use; all except one were biplanes. The weather on both the first and succeeding days was poor with a wind blowing frequent gusts but, despite this, there were 21 starters, although this number was steadily reduced by retirements as the course took its toll. The winner was finally Captain Franklin L. Barnard, the former war pilot who was to become better known as Commodore of the Instone Air Line which flew from Croydon as the air division of the Instone shipping group, in Sir Samuel Instone's DH4A. The average speed was 126.6 mph with a flying time of 6 hours, 32 minutes and 50 seconds with F.P. Raynham in a gaudily-finished black and yellow Martinsyde F6 coming second and the later-renowned A.J. Cobham in a DH9B being placed third.

At the time of the presentation of the Cup there had been some strong feeling that, although it was such a large and handsome trophy, a new one should be awarded annually and it should not be presented on a challenge basis. This was agreed by the time of the race the following year, since it was felt that in this way His Majesty's original suggestion that it would act as an encouragement to sporting flying, would best be realised.

During the burial of Britain's Unknown Warrior on Armistice Day, 1920, the same Soldier at whose homecoming the guns of Dover Castle had fired 19 rounds so that a distinguished journalist had remarked 'A Field Marshal's salute for poor old "Tommy"—that would have surprised him', Prince Albert had walked in the cortège in the uniform of a Wing Commander. Now, however, two years later, it was noted at such public events as the betrothal of his sister to Viscount Lascelles that he wore the insignia of a Group Captain. It was about this time that saw the introduction of a new ceremonial head-dress for Royal Air Force officers and one of the first occasions on which Prince Albert wore one was when new Colours were presented to the Brigade of Guards by George V in July, although the very first was probably in Waterloo Place, Pall Mall, exactly a year before, during the unveiling of the statue of the earlier king who had encouraged the advance of aviation, Edward VII. The only reason why this item of dress is mentioned here is in order to record the Prince's personal dislike of this hat, no doubt due to its strange resemblance to nothing so much as a crash-helmet partly covered in fur with a front plume. In future years after he had ascended the throne, the Prince, now King George VI, made is abundantly clear to the Air Council that any full dress uniform introduced after the 1939-45 war must include something different in the manner of head-gear!

The irritations such as princes, no less than the rest of us have to bear, apart, there is no doubting the genuine regard for the Service of his adoption that Prince Albert showed. He had re-visited his old station at Cranwell in Lincolnshire some time before and found much that had changed since the days of its Naval use for it had now been opened as a College on a par with Sandhurst and Dartmouth, although long years were still to pass before the main building was opened for use in September 1933.

Meanwhile, the end of 1922 brought a new rank to another of the Royal princes and, in December, the *London Gazette* contained the announcement that His Majesty the King had been pleased to approve the appointment of: 'His Royal Highness Edward Albert Christian George Andrew Patrick David, Prince of Wales and Duke of Cornwall, KG, KT, GCSI, GCMG, GCIE, GCVO, GBE, MC, to be a Group Captain in the Royal Air Force'.

The following year, 1923, was neither full, nor eventful from a viewpoint of Royal encouragement of aviation and the newspapers were much more occupied with such events as the French entry into the Ruhr, the disorder and the policeman on the white horse at the Wembley Cup Final, the decay of the old Waterloo Bridge and the re-building of Regent Street. But there were some events worthy of recording in the aviation press of the day, including the attendance at the RAF Pageant at Hendon of King George V and Queen Mary in the company of Air Vice-Marshal J.F.A. Higgins and the Duke and Duchess of York.

Making rather a wider public impact were the ceremonies during the same month at the top of Whitehall Stairs on the Victoria Embankment when the 54-foot tall RAF Memorial was unveiled by the Prince of Wales in the companionship of his brother Albert, in RAF uniform. Part of this project organised by the Royal Air Force Benevolent Fund had been supported by an exhibition of aircraft paintings which had also received the patronage of the Royal Family. Quite naturally, the latter Prince had, in the eyes of the public, taken a large part of the limelight on this occasion for, as recently as the end of April, he had been married on a rather grey, damp morning with the relief of faint sunshine only later, to the petite and pretty Lady Elizabeth Bowes Lyon from Scotland. For this historic ceremony the groom had once again worn the uniform of his chosen Service.

The following summer had been marked for many, especially at Southampton, by the visit to the Supermarine Aviation Works there of the Prince of Wales. The occasion saw the Prince introduced to a number of the senior staff including one, Reginald J. Mitchell, the Chief Engineer of the company. No one could know at the time that the event was to have deeply historical overtones for shaking hands were the two men who would, in the fullness of time, become innovators in the field of aviation, one to be the architect of the Royal Flight, the other to design the 'Spitfire' fighter.

From a strictly military point of view the same year was to have more immediate impact, however, for, also during July, there took place an important pioneer use of aircraft at the royal review of the Navy at Spithead. This was the first that had taken place for ten years and between the fateful summer of 1914 and the present late July day had come the holocaust of what was then known as the Great War. Then, the naval air participation had been slight, little more than the exhibition of moored seaplanes at the entrance to the harbour at Portsmouth but now the role of aeroplanes was much more active and as the Royal yacht, *Victoria and Albert,* had steamed slowly between the lines of warships off Spithead, totalling some 200 vessels, it had been escorted by aircraft overhead making a brave sight against the backdrop of a blue sky provided by an exceptionally fine day. By now too, Royal attendance at the RAF Pageant had become a regular sight and when the Duke and Duchess of York had arrived at Hendon that Saturday, in July, in the company of the same Duke of Connaught, a son of Queen Victoria, who had witnessed the naming ceremony for the ASC Sopwith Camel, their party had included His Majesty the King of Denmark.

The former wartime equipment of the RAF had now largely vanished and in its place were appearing new machines for the first line of defence which embodied the technological advances of the time; a fact reflected on the cover by A.B. Cree for the 1925 RAF Display programme showing Armstrong-Whitworth Siskins over Mark I-type tanks. These changes were real as well as imaginary, however, and this was shown by a happening at that event involving no less than George V himself.

Squadron Leader A.H. Peck had taken into the air nine Gloster Grebes of No 25 Squadron from Hawkinge, a type they had only taken on strength in October the year before. Meanwhile, George V had been invited to seat himself at an oak desk looking strangely out of place in the surroundings of an airfield. In front of his Majesty was a strange wooden box with a perforated front; a microphone no less, for the fighters now in formation over the aerodrome were equipped with radio telephones by means of which it was possible to speak to the pilots in flight. The event was intended to be an exhibition of squadron drill, by which means it was believed that any battles in the sky of the future would be fought and, as an illustration of the ease whereby a controller might henceforth command his men from the ground, the King was to issue the orders to his men.

'Hello Mosquitoes', the gruff but kindly voice of George V crackled into the flyers' headphones as the King leant forward on his stick towards the box as if to ensure he be heard. 'Hello Mosquitoes, alter course 16 points outwards.' An expectant hush had fallen on the watchers as they strained their eyes upwards; then the move took place and the nine little buzzing biplanes moved across the sky in obedience to the King's words: a small event but, by the standards of the day, a portentous one, yet only a few of the watchers knew they were witnessing the making of history.

The displays of RAF precision at Hendon always contained evidence of some new advance in the march of aeronautical progress, but when these were demonstrated to the Royal Family they tended to claim the interest of the public to a more marked degree. An example of this was to take place in 1926 when the RAF station north of London was visited on Display day, not only by the King and Queen, but also King Alfonso and the Queen of Spain, while also among the visitors might be found Sir

Hugh Trenchard, Sir Geoffrey Salmond and, further evidence of the Spanish royal interest, the inventor of the Autogyro, Juan de la Cierva.

During the year before, the first British Autogyro had been constructed to an Air Ministry order and now the Cierva Autogyro Company Limited had been promoted in this country. Naturally, an example of such a machine, based on the fuselage of the ubiquitous Avro 504, was exhibited in the New Types Park at Hendon, and the pilot detailed to demonstrate the type was Frank T. Courtney, a well-known figure in aviation.

In order to ensure a trouble-free performance the machine had been sent up for testing the previous day and an uneventful flight and landing took place. Then, without warning, as the machine came to rest, the rotor blades which should have slowly ceased to revolve and remain horizontal when at rest, displayed a marked reluctance to do anything of the sort and, still revolving, drooped lower and lower until they began to be truncated to the sound of splintering wood as they were consumed by the spinning propeller! What had happened was that the fitting at the head of the rotor assembly that anchored the wires when at rest had come away in flight so that once centrifugal force was exhausted the blades dropped into what may be called an amputation angle.

The effect on the demonstrators, anxious to show the new craft to the King the next day, may well be imagined while to cap it all, the pilot who had won the King's Cup in a cleaned-up Armstrong-Whitworth Siskin in 1923, the second year of the contest, appeared to be lying dead on the ground, felled by a piece of timber from the disintegrating blades.

The first sign that things might not be as bad as they first appeared was when the 'corpse' of Frank Courtney slowly staggered to its feet and, during the subsequent inspection of the airframe, it became evident that the spare set of rotor blades could probably be fixed if time allowed. If was now late afternoon, but the decision was taken to work all night on the job in an effort to get it done. All went well and the next day, the crowd and the Royal visitors, who included the Duke of York, were treated to a display of flying a rotary-winged machine that could not have been bettered. After the final landing had been made by the immaculate silver machine with its black nose and prominent identification number '16' on the side, King George came forward and held out his hand to congratulate the pilot. But to the minds of those within earshot leapt the question whether the King knew more of the events of the previous 24 hours than he deemed it expedient to admit, for the remark from His Majesty that they overheard was on the lines of a belief that a living might possibly be made in a less hazardous manner!

There was no question now that the art and science of aviation was far greater than a duty interest to several members of the Royal Family. In the light of this fact it is no surprise that, as the 1920s drew to their close, it was to be the Prince of Wales, who had shown such a genuine aptitude as a pilot in the final months of the First World War, who would take the first step to establish what was to evolve into what is today the Queen's Flight.

By the spring of 1928, King George V had seen plenty of flying since the days nine years before when he had counselled his eldest son to fly no more, when matters had come to a head following the bizarre trip with Major Barker, VC. And, although there is no doubt that the King had come to like aviation no more than in the earlier days (and, indeed, it is a fact that he never flew personally throughout his life) his attitude had changed sufficiently to realise that aviation was now no more dangerous than the risks on the polo field, a point of view no doubt slowly realised as his experience as the father of four surviving vigorous young men widened.

The first flight taken by the Prince of Wales enjoying his new freedom took place on April 27 and the aircraft involved was once more a Bristol Fighter. The particular machine was flown by Flying Officer G.C. Stemp of the Communications Flight of No 24 Squadron from Northolt whence it had moved from Hendon during January of the year before.

The historic trip in question had lasted no more than 30 minutes in a machine numbered J8430 and not only did it mark a new series of events that were to reach unbroken down the years to the present age; it also established the long association with the British Royal Family that 24 Squadron was to enjoy for many years.

This time there was encountered no parental opposition but instead, only two weeks later, authority was granted for the Flight to be augmented by one additional machine. At the time the establishment was for two Avro 504Ns, two de Havilland 'Moths' and five Bristol F2B Fighters, and it was to this latter group that was added one more of the type, in fact J8430 again, 'For Special Service'.

In the history of the Royal Air Force this was the first time that a special aircraft had been introduced in permanent establishment for what would today be termed VIP uses but it was not a pioneer move in the use of aeroplanes in the carriage of important persons for this had begun on a temporary basis many years before. The precedent had been established not for royal persons but for the ferrying of delegates in connection with the Versailles Peace Conference as far back as 1919 when, in the Hall of Mirrors under the inscribed boast of an earlier unconstitutional monarch, *'Le Roi gouverne pour lui-même'*—'The King governs on his own'—that the politicians had attempted to hammer out an honourable peace from the carnage of the war.

Machines used on this forerunner of anything approaching a Royal Flight had been de Havilland 4As and Handley Page 0/400s, formerly wartime bombers, with the first type being mainly employed for the conveyance of despatches. In this work their base nearest to the British Capital had been Kenley aerodrome, established at first as an Aircraft Acceptance Park on the common land forming part of the Surrey Downs in 1917, and the aircraft and crews had been formed into an official Communications Wing for the work in connection with the Peace Conference.

In this the lighter machines were not unlike those used at about the same time for the conveyance of Forces' mail between Belgium, France, Luxemburg and Germany, a measure set up jointly and at great speed by Major E.E. Gawthorn of the Royal Engineers Postal Section, Lieutenant Colonel H. Blackburn of the RAF and Colonel D.J. Lidbury of the General Post Office.

Inevitably, former war planes were used for the service, de Havilland 9As with 400 hp Liberty motors, each of which bore a printed notice over the instrument panel with a strange warning. It read: 'Do not open the throttle more than two thirds under 6,000 ft'. The unstated reason was that such was the force of the slipstream that it was quite capable of damaging the tail unit if not kept under proper control!

Enough has been said to prove that it was for commoners, not kings, that the idea of special duties aircraft was introduced. Since it was regarded as only an interim machine, the alterations from the standard Bristol Fighter carried out on J8430 were few, but they included a special rear cockpit in place of the Scarff ring and, although the VIP standard included the fitting of a very large windshield and a rear fairing to give a small increase in depth, the occupant still had to wear complete leather flying clothing in order to endure the rigours of the trip. The Handley Page slots on the leading edge of the upper wings were, by now, a standard fitting and the only other indication of the special use of the Bristol was the high, mirror-like finish given to the metal panels of the cowling and immediately forward of the front cockpit.

The first use of this historic aeroplane took place on May 27 1928 when an official flight was made from Scarborough race course to Bircham Newton after the attendance of Prince Edward at the annual conference of the British Legion. This had been followed by an impressive service of remembrance at the War Memorial on Oliver's Mount, Scarborough, which was also attended by Lady Haig, Marshal Foch and Lord Jellicoe. When this ceremony was over the Prince was taken by car to the race course where Squadron Leader J.S. Don waited with the silver Bristol. The Royal machine was escorted throughout the flight that followed by another machine of the same type, J6681, piloted by the same Flying Officer Stemp who had taken the Prince to renew his air experience on April 27, but this time his passenger was Captain Ogilvy.

Only three days later the same pair of machines, with the same pilots, were once more pressed into service for Royal duties when the Prince opened Eaton Park, Norwich. For this work he had been

The first official royal aeroplane—Bristol F2B, J8430, at Mousehold airfield, Norwich, 1928, with the Prince of Wales climbing aboard. He is wearing complete flying kit and a parachute.

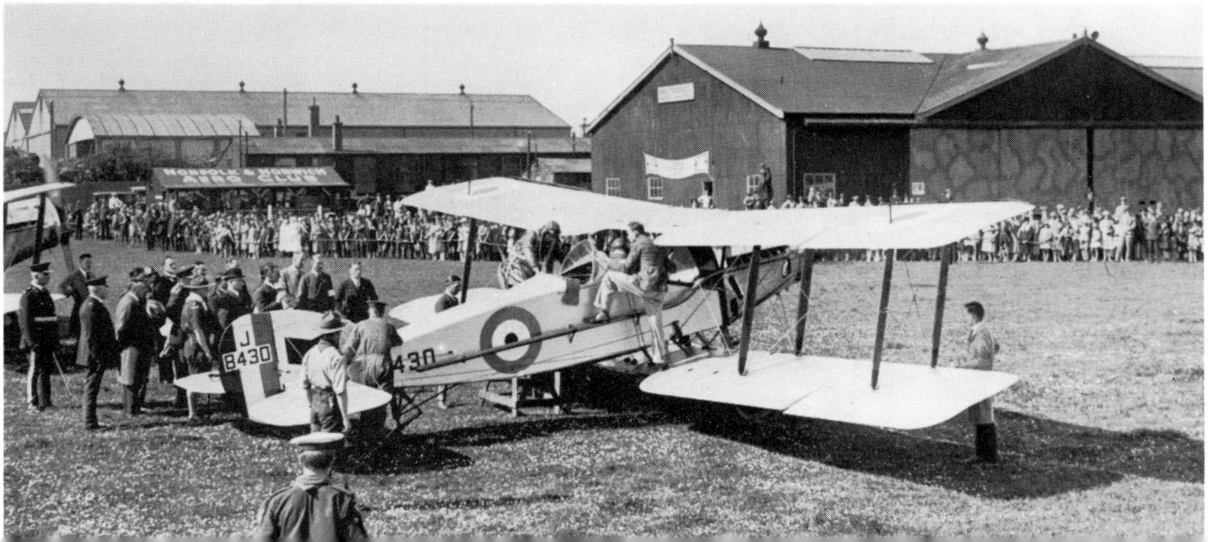

accompanied by Brigadier Trotter in the second machine and the landing ground had been Mousehold Aerodrome. Before leaving for Northolt, Prince Edward had also taken the opportunity to visit the Norfolk and Norwich Aero Club which had its club house alongside the Boulton & Paul aircraft sheds, still bearing on their doors the colours of the disruptive camouflage applied in the days of their wartime service.

It was probably felt at the time, quite rightly many agreed, that the use of semi-obsolete machines of the same pattern that had been used over the trenches of Flanders and elsewhere were hardly fitting as transports for a national ambassador and so steps were taken to replace the Bristol Fighter temporarily on charge with a more up to date type. This was forthcoming in the delivery on June 26 1928 to Northolt RAF Station of the first of a pair of special Westland Wapiti biplanes, J9096, while a second, J9095, was flown in the following day. These machines were designated Mark IAs and differed from standard only in having the rear Scarff rings replaced by normal cockpits, open in the manner of the day. Apart from this there was nothing to distinguish them from the standard aircraft of the type already in use by day-bomber squadrons as a General Purpose machine. This had been designed as a replacement for the de Havilland 9A incorporating, it was directed, in an attempt to restrict the public spending of the day, as many parts of the earlier machine as possible.

Despite the presence of the new air aircraft on the establishment of No 24 Squadron, the Bristol Fighter was not immediately dispensed with and Prince Edward was to make his final trip in it on July 18. This was the occasion of his visit to Grimsby where his engagement consisted of an inspection of the Armament Practice Station, and for this a landing had been made at North Coates.

However, although the new machines of the Wapiti type had not yet carried their Royal passenger it is not to say that they had lain unused for these aircraft had been employed for work that was to establish another precedent that is true of the Queen's Flight to this day. There is no claim that the unit be reserved for the exclusive use of Royalty and such an arrangement has never existed, a fact proven by the realisation that the machines attached to the Communications Flight had been employed to carry the Chief of Air Staff, the Under Secretary of State for Air and even the Prime Minister himself that year before the special aircraft had ever been used to carry the Prince.

As 1928 drew towards its close the aircraft was used to a lessening degree as autumn set in and Prince Edward had gone abroad on the second of his African tours. While on safari he had found himself at Khartoum, the base of No 47 Squadron. They were flying another two-seater General Purpose type, one of the mainstays of the RAF in those days, the Fairey IIIF, and the Prince seized the first chance that presented itself to visit the squadron and gain some experience as a passenger in the type. At first it appeared that this was no more than the indulgence of his personal enthusiasm for aviation, but in point of fact it was to have important results at a slightly later date.

Westland Wapiti Mk IA J9095, one of a pair converted for royal use. Note the No 24 Squadron chevron on the fin.

Meanwhile, plans were being organized for what was to be the longest flight to be made by a Royal aircraft up to that time; this was to take the form of a journey to Copenhagen, in order to bring back to this country the Duke of York, who was on an official visit to Denmark. The outward trip on October 19 passed without incident and the sight of a British military machine in Scandinavia excited much comment. The fin was adorned with the red chevron common to all the No 24 Squadron aircraft and by now some small marks of its use had been painted on to the airframe in the form of a miniature Group Captain's rank pennant at the mid-point of each of the outer pair of interplane struts.

However, as events would have it, bad weather with a rolling mist reducing the visibility to a dangerously low limit, prevented Prince Albert using an aircraft to return home and it was decided that the better plan was for him to go by sea. Squadron Leader Don was forced to wait at Copenhagen for several days until the weather cleared sufficiently for him to fly the Wapiti, J9095, home once more.

Scarcely three weeks later there took place one of those relatively new royal duties that had come about as a result of the Great War and, on November 11, King George led his subjects in the poignant annual homage to the Nation's dead. In those days it was marked by ceremonies that stilled the entire land, even on a working day when all activity ceased at the eleventh hour. On these occasions the King and his sons would stand bareheaded within a little wooden stockade in Whitehall beside the Cenotaph to observe the two minutes' silence. The chill November morning in 1928 was made more unpleasant by the driving rain and, a few days later, His Majesty had taken to his bed with a slight, feverish cold.

By the beginning of the following month his condition had not improved at all but was, in fact, giving cause for anxiety as the fever was affecting his lungs, and on Sunday, December 2, special prayers were said in churches throughout the country for the King's recovery. At the same time, Edward, Prince of Wales was in Africa but so grave was the news that reached him from Buckingham Palace, that the tour was cut short. He was rushed to London where he found great, silent crowds thronging the approach to the palace where the latest bulletin on his father's condition was exhibited on a board beside the gates where it would be read aloud by the few near enough to do so for the benefit of the majority behind.

Throughout December the strange ritual continued although the crowds grew smaller, for two days after the climax of his illness a more hopeful message had appeared. It read: 'The King has passed a quieter night. Though the anxiety concerning the heart must continue, the improvement noted last evening is so far satisfactorily maintained. (Signed) Stanley Hewett. Dawson of Penn. 10.30 am, 4th December 1928'.

This crisis in the dying month of the year may at first seem to have little to do with aviation, but that such is not the case is shown by reference to the chain of events in the New Year, for January was marked by the removal of the royal patient to the south coast. The journey through London was made in an ambulance with no blinds over the windows so that the crowds might catch a glimpse of the frail-looking, bearded figure within, bound for convalescence at Bognor, a town henceforth to be known at Bognor Regis.

In order to economise in the all-too-short days that were now the lot of the Prince of Wales as a result of the King's illness, it was not long into the spring that it was realised that with the RAF Station at Tangmere lying not far from the town, the obvious answer to the question of travel seemed to be to resort to the air. Consequently, as soon as the weather improved the royal Westland Wapiti machines were once more pressed into service and the Prince made the first of two trips to Bognor to visit his now-recovering father on April 3; actually flying in J9095 with Squadron Leader Don at the controls, while Flight Lieutenant Stemp, a second name now increasingly familiar in connection with royal flights, provided escort in J9096.

Princes to Act

'A kingdom for a stage, princes to act,
And monarchs to behold the swelling scene!'
Henry V, William Shakespeare

It seemed almost that Prince Edward's use of the aeroplane to visit his father ushered in a new era for the Royal Family, for there followed a series of flying visits to different parts of the country using the nearest available landing ground to the destination, the journey being completed by road as had been done in April from Tangmere to Craigwell, Bognor Regis. These two important trips also established the pattern that was to be followed for some time, namely the second aircraft, if not used to convey an equerry perhaps, was still flown solo to provide an escort.

As the summer advanced with its better flying weather, still of paramount importance for the aircraft of the day, more royal trips by air took place. One such was carried out on June 13 1929 when the two special Wapitis from No 24 Squadron flew to Manston in order that Prince Edward might attend the RAF's annual athletic meeting at Sandwich. On July 23, Squadron Leader Don was once more taking the Prince to a celebration, this time landing at Bass Meadows, Burton-on-Trent, where the royal visitor had been invited to attend the town's Jubilee celebrations, and 1929 saw also similar trips to such scattered destinations as Bircham Newton, Castle Bromwich and Hooton.

As might be expected in any forward-looking man, journeys such as these were not long in kindling a desire in the Prince to be a participant rather than merely a passenger, for it is necessary to remind ourselves that at this time he was only 35 years of age and had seen man's successful conquest of flight when he was a bright boy of nine. Thus that September saw him become the owner of his own aeroplane. The type chosen was a de Havilland DH60M Gipsy Moth registered G-AALG which was fitted with full dual controls and a refinement regarded as the last word in comfort at the time—pneumatic upholstery, inflatable seating that was to be found a little later in the ubiquitous Austin Seven car.

It might be imagined that the purchase of an aeroplane would bring the young prince into conflict with King George V in the light of the fact that His Majesty had, only a little earlier, counselled his son to refrain from indulging in the dangers of steeplechasing. But despite the fact that Prince Edward had openly requested Squadron Leader Don to give him flying lessons, the King raised no objection when the course of instruction was begun and it was found that the passage of time since his air experience at Waddon at the end of the Great War had done nothing to diminish the genuine natural talent for flying that Prince Edward enjoyed.

At the same time, the royal brothers, Henry, Duke of Gloucester and George, Duke of Kent, also took flying tuition and, quite naturally a friendly rivalry developed between the three royal brothers as to which of them would go solo first. The pattern of instruction followed the established course for each of the three, with several hours dual and the inevitable 'circuits and bumps'. But, in the case of Prince Edward, the latter were surprisingly few and unusually light. His natural aptitude ensured that one summer's evening Squadron Leader Don was to climb from the brightly-finished Moth in its Brigade of Guards colours at Northolt, reach back inside and remove the second control column from in front of the red leather-covered seat and waved the Prince off for his first solo with two landings of which the second was distinctly inferior to the first! This was no doubt due to the state of excitement that Prince Edward was in and it has been recorded that his elation was such that he wasted no time in telephoning his brothers to announce 'I've beaten you to it!' and probably added a claim to the five pound bet which, he seemed to remember in after years, was his due from the other Princes.

Having established that he was a sound pilot, the Prince of Wales was content to allow a Service officer to fly him in future and this duty was nearly always performed by David Don. Typical of the journeys by air was that made at the beginning of September, when the royal Moth went to Cowes in order that the teams gathered for the Schneider Trophy Contest might be visited. During his visit to the Calshot RAF Station, the Prince was photographed with the Italian and British teams before being flown over the course on September 3 in an RAF Supermarine Southampton flying boat.

However, the position with regard to a Service pilot flying the Prince on private journeys brought about complications from a purely practical standpoint, since the Squadron Leader could not always be released from his duties with No 24 Squadron, a position further complicated by the fact that he was needed to fly squadron machines during official visits. In addition, when it was necessary to carry out the normal pre-flight check routine, there were difficulties when a Service pilot was flying a privately-owned machine, for the Gipsy Moth was still the personal property of the Prince.

The solution was, obviously, for the appointment of a full-time personal pilot and enquiries were begun to discover a suitable candidate. It was then that assistance came from an unexpected source which was to establish the long chain of events that was to result in the formation of a special Flight and its resultant descendant today.

An eminent politician of the day was the Right Honourable Frederick Guest who was a personal friend of both Lloyd George and Winston Churchill. Not only had he been at one time the Minister for Air but was still a keen aviator who owned a private Junkers aircraft and employed a personal pilot. This pilot had flown Guest over much of Europe and the Middle East and the two had assisted in blazing pioneer trails in parts of Africa, so that it was a very experienced man that the politician had in mind when, one day in 1929 he approached the Prince of Wales with the words, 'I'm going to let you have my pilot'.

The man in question was the son of a doctor who had been born 26 years before, in December 1903, at Bracknell near Ascot, where he had received the first part of his education at Heatherdown before going on to Malvern College. On leaving there, young Edward H. Fielden had entered the Royal Air Force in 1924 and had obtained a short service commission before being posted to No 23 Squadron, freshly equipped with Gloster Gamecock fighters at Henlow in 1926, after a period flying the Gloster Grebes of No 25 from Hawkinge in the previous year.

With the former unit he had been a member of its aerobatic team in company with R.L.R. 'Batchy' Atcherly who, as a Flying Officer, was a member of the Schneider Trophy Team representing Great Britain in 1929. In September 1926, Fielden had been posted to the Station Flight at Duxford and it was here that he was given a chance to show his capabilities as a pilot. The Duxford Station Flight sought to maintain an unbroken record of daily operations irrespective of the weather conditions and, in order to keep this unchanged, only pilots of the highest calibre were selected for the work, since to do it called for not only a very high degree of technical skill but also an enthusiasm and determination above average.

However, after the termination of the five years associated with the type of commission which Edward Fielden held, he was transferred to the Reserve of Royal Air Force Officers with the rank of Flight Lieutenant and he began to seek out a new career in civil aviation despite the somewhat bleak prospects which existed in this, as in the Service field of the day.

Despite his reputation for precision flying which had earned him the award of an Air Force Cross, and a tendency to be a perfectionist in matters mechanical, he was a man of quiet reserve and this had quickly gained him the nick-name of 'Mouse' during his school days which persisted for the remainder of his life. Nevertheless it denoted qualities which, allied to his ability as an administrator, were to combine with his skill as a

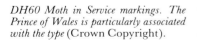

DH60 Moth in Service markings. The Prince of Wales is particularly associated with the type (Crown Copyright).

pilot to make him the seemingly ideal candidate for a unique post in the years to come.

The new duties of Prince Edward's personal pilot included full responsibility for the servicing and maintenance of the Gipsy Moth as well as acting as its sole pilot. In addition he also assumed responsibility for the further training of the Duke of Gloucester and the Duke of Kent as pilots, so that the post was a demanding one. Official flights were, however, still made in a Service machine and this still meant a Wapiti with an RAF officer to fly it. For journeys of this nature an official rota was compiled consisting of the names of three pilots with, at the head, that of Squadron Leader David Don once more. But even here, Fielden's influence was felt for it appears that shortly after taking up his appointment certain improvements were carried out to J9095 under his direction.

This particular 'special service' machine was to come in for extended use as 1929 drew towards its close for, not only was the Prince of Wales to use aircraft as a means of transport to lighten and extend royal duties, but it was also used to transport his brothers. In this connection Prince George was to use Wapiti J9095 twice during the year, once being the occasion when he was picked up from Smith's Lawn on September 10, the Windsor sward now being marked out for use as a landing ground by the erection of a windsock.

The following year was a very full one for the royal brothers and their enthusiasm for aviation, not only because it was the year in which the two younger members of the group completed their flying training but also because 1930 marked the acquisition of three aircraft by Prince Edward. The Gipsy Moth G-AALG was still in use and this was added to by another of the same type, G-ABCW. But this machine was to suffer a mishap on July 18 so that it was replaced by a de Havilland DH60X, G-ABDB, and was joined by a dual control DH84 Puss Moth, thus representing not only the first monoplane bought by the Prince but also the first use of a cabin machine.

Before these events had taken place, however, their royal owner once again found himself in Africa from which he had been obliged to depart so suddenly when his father's illness reached its crisis. Here, he had put in some additional hours in a Gipsy Moth at Nairobi, not his own machine but one belonging to the distinguished record-breaking pilot of the day, Tom Campbell Black, a name later to be associated with that of C.W.A. Scott and the DH88 Comet racer which won the air race to Australia from Mildenhall.

The end of the African tour was to be marked by one of the longest royal trips by air attempted up to that time and for this the Wapiti J9095 was once again employed. The departure from Africa had been made via Port Said in the SS *Rawlpindi* which finally arrived on April 25 at Marseilles. From here it was planned to complete the journey to England by air. The pilot on this occasion, since a Service aircraft was involved, was once again David Don, now a Member of the Victorian Order since the New Year Honours had been published, in recognition of his services to the Prince. As on previous occasions, J9096 was used as an escort with Flight Lieutenant H.W. Heslop at the controls and with Colonel Puris Leigh in the second seat. Naturally the endurance of even military aircraft at that time was somewhat limited and stops were made for refuelling at Lyons and Le Bourget.

In fact, although the journey to France had been made in the P&O liner, a previous stage of the trip home had been carried out by air for, on April 13, an RAF Fairey IIIF had been used by the Prince to make the journey from Malakal to Khartoum with a stop *en route* at Kosi. The journey was completed on April 17 when Cairo was reached after a trip that had begun the day before, following a route which took in Wadi Halfa and Assuan.

It is of interest to note the type of machine that was employed in the light of subsequent events, and it was one of this type that was the third machine to fly from Marseilles, piloted by Flying Officer J.W. Pearson-Rogers. All three machines left Northolt on April 22, arriving in France with a sufficient margin to meet the liner on April 24, and making Marignane aerodrome their temporary base.

Departure with the Prince on board one of the Wapitis had been made at 7.35 am and the journey to the first refuelling station, a distance of 175 miles, was completed in exactly an hour and a half. Twenty-five minutes later the three once again took off and the stop-over at Le Bourget was lengthened in order to include lunch. Take off for the final leg of the journey was made at 1.45 pm and escort was provided by nine machines of the Armée de l'Air under Capitaine Lackeman. At the French coast these turned for home and their place was taken by a British flying boat which remained with the formation during its 15-minute journey across the Channel.

Once over English soil its place was taken by a further nine machines, this time Armstrong Whitworth Siskins of No 25 Squadron, flying from Hawkinge, and these remained in position until Windsor was reached. Meanwhile, the other two aircraft had left the group for their bases leaving the Prince's Wapiti to make landfall on Smith's Lawn at 4 pm, the venue at Windsor being described in some contemporary reports alternatively as

'Canadian Camp'. The total flying time for the 650 mile journey was 6 hours, 10 minutes at an average speed, and this was commented on at the time, of 105 mph.

The following summer saw the Duke of Gloucester make use of the same Wapiti on June 5 when he made a visit to Duxford, but a new type appeared in the Prince of Wales' log-book, recording his visit to launch a new RNLI lifeboat at Dover, to be named the *Sir William Hilliary.* This fresh aircraft was the first of a batch of elementary trainers, Hawker Tomtit, J9772. On this occasion it appears that the usual roles were reversed and when the little biplane landed at Dover, the pilot was the Prince and the Squadron Leader was in the second seat as passenger. It is also interesting to note that touch-down was made on the old aerodrome at Swingate, Dover, the same spot, high above sea level on the cliffs which, as Swingate Downs had seen, the first four squadrons of the Royal Flying Corps assembled to depart for France in August 1914 at the outbreak of the First World War.

Only a fortnight after the royal landing at Dover in the machine from, once again, No 24 Squadron, a second Tomtit enters the picture. This time it was a civil machine, G-AALL, which had been lent to the Prince by the Hawker Aircraft company for entry into the King's Cup Air Race, and the pilot was to be David Don. This explains why it was he and not Edward Fielden who now normally flew his royal namesake in civil machines and was in charge of the Tomtit when it was intended to fly to Caernarvon. But, despite it being the month of June, the weather closed in and a landing had to be made at Castle Bromwich. Startled officials were surprised to see the heir to the throne step from a machine already prominently bearing the racing number 33 *en route* for an official visit which, in this particular event, had to be cancelled since the Prince returned to London in the aircraft.

Although he had put in some hours in another DH60X, belonging to 'Freddie' Guest, Flight Lieutenant Fielden's former employer, the Prince of Wales had available all the air transport he might immediately need since he was the owner of three aircraft. Indeed the possession of these was creating something of a problem at Northolt. It was therefore decided that the trio be transferred to Hendon since not only was this the base for the Service machines used for official trips but also it was a simple matter for the machines to be accommodated under the same conditions as those permitting serving officers to maintain personal civil aircraft there. The Prince came into this category by virtue of the fact that, with effect from September 1 1930, he had been promoted to the rank of Air Chief Marshal, having previously been a Group Captain.

Once at Hendon, and stored in the Display Hangar, it was a simpler matter for Flight Lieutenant Fielden to care for the aircraft, obtaining fuel and lubricants etc from the RAF stores, although all these items had to be privately paid for and in no way were these private machines maintained at public expense. Meanwhile official journeys were being made in special Service machines with a group of pilots authorised to fly them still headed by Squadron Leader David S. Don, MVO, and including Flight Lieutenants H.W. Heslop and J.D.G. Armour. It was perhaps to distinguish the Service aircraft earmarked for the Prince's use that his private collection about this time began to be referred to, quite unofficially, as the 'Royal Flight'.

Shortly before this the equipment of No 24 Squadron for royal use had been changed and the end of the summer had seen the Wapitis replaced by two of the type that had contributed to the Prince of Wales' air experience earlier in the year, the Fairey IIIF. The first of these had been joined the next day by a second, making K1115 and J9061 the new official pair. These differed in some details from the No 47 Squadron aircraft in which the Prince had been flown from Malakal to Khartoum by Flight Lieutenant A.B. Bowen-Buscarlet, in that the rear

J9772, the Hawker Tomtit in which Prince Edward flew to Dover in 1930 (Crown Copyright).

seat was equipped to VIP standards. As yet the special cabin still lay in the future and, as a result, it was not uncommon to see the heir to the throne on those occasions when protocol could be disregarded, step down from an aeroplane in a flying helmet and a none-too-well pressed long overcoat to protect him from the elements, with a parachute uncomfortably strapped on top.

One of the earliest uses of K1115 had been to visit the Antwerp Exhibition, but more exciting was the trip on August 13, during a series of visits to RAF stations at the time of the Annual Air Exercises. For purposes of these manoeuvres the country was divided into two parts termed 'Redland' and 'Blueland' with each sector protected by patrolling interceptors. It was one of these, a flight of Armstrong Whitworth Siskin fighters, that suddenly spotted a strange Fairey IIIF crossing their area. Without hesitation the leader swung his formation into simulated attacks. The thrill of being at the receiving end of this harassment delighted the Prince whose only disappointment was that Squadron Leader Don refused to be driven from his course and showed no inclination to take the appropriate evasive action. In fact he was only obeying orders for the C-in-C Inland Area had laid down very strict rules for the royal pilots which forbade them indulging in any 'dangerous' aerobatics with the Prince of Wales on board, although there is no doubt that both young men, pilot and passenger, would have enjoyed something more to their liking than the dull routine of 'straight and level'.

Among the duties of Edward Fielden was the assumption of responsibility to complete the flying training of the other two Princes, George and Henry. The first of these was the Duke of Gloucester who went solo on June 22 to be followed a little later by his younger brother, the Duke of Kent, on October 12, and it was not long before the two became 'private owners' when they jointly bought shares in G-ABDB, the Gipsy Moth.

In November 1930, Prince Edward had a chance to indulge his private interest in the developments that were taking place in the science of aviation for that month saw the arrival, at Southampton Water, of one of the wonders of the age at that time, the massive, 12-engined Dornier Do X flying boat. In order to travel down to the south coast, the Prince embarked at Hendon in the twin-motor Saro Cloud a 64-foot span high-wing monoplane with a metal hull and accommodation for nine, including the pilot. This was to be the Prince's first experience of an amphibian and, having taken off from the grass at Hendon, G-ABCJ made a smooth touch-down on the sea off Calshot. From here a transfer was made to the German flying boat which took off for a brief flight with the Prince seated next to the pilot.

Once in the air the 55-ton machine, with its top speed of 130 mph given by the tandem set of 550 hp Curtiss Conquerors, handled well and, almost inevitably, the Prince's enthusiasm came to the fore and it was not long before he was at the controls and remained in charge of the huge machine for fully ten minutes. After returning to the less-spacious cabin of the Saro machine he blinked in mock surprise before turning to those in his party with the cryptic remark 'It's shrunk!'

The main event of the royal year in 1931 was a tour of South America by Prince Edward who set off in the company of Prince George. This meant the first of a new set of responsibilities for Flight Lieutenant Fielden since he had to plan the aviation side of the trip which included arrangements to take the Puss Moth out to Buenos Aires in HMS *Eagle.* The details of this plan were complicated by the fact that thc royal brothers wished to make the first part of the journey by air, flying G-ABBS to Le Bourget from where they were to go to Santander in Spain, there to board SS *Oropesa* for the voyage to the Americas. Eventually the problems were solved by the decision to take a new Puss Moth direct from England in the aircraft carrier while the old G-ABBS was to be returned to this country and sold. The DH60 was not the only item of an aeronautical nature on the naval vessel since, as the visit had its commercial overtones in that some British exhibits were destined for the International Exhibition, a visit to which was included in the Princes' itinerary, the cargo included several items for display on the aviation industry's stands at Buenos Aires.

While abroad, the Prince of Wales lost no opportunity of widening his experience of flying and managed to fit into his schedule a trip in another amphibian, this time a Sikorsky, a Ford Tri-motor and a Supermarine Southampton, similar to that in which he had toured the Schneider Trophy course off Cowes, but this time operated by the Argentine Navy. In addition he made a new type of flight in a Fairey IIIF, since it was at this time that the first royal landing was carried out on the deck of an aircraft carrier when he visited HMS *Eagle,* although the experience of a take off from a vessel had to wait until July 12 1932 when Prince Edward flew from the deck of HMS *Courageous* during the Royal Review of the Fleet.

The return home for the Prince of Wales was made through France and this occasioned the use of the largest aircraft used for royalty up to that time, in the form of a chartered Armstrong Whitworth Argosy, one of the big three-motored biplanes operated on scheduled services by Imperial

Airways. The actual machine chosen was the *City of Glasgow* with Captain Gordon Olley, later to found Olley Airways, of Croydon, at the controls.

The trip from Lisbon to Bordeaux, where the airliner was already waiting, had been made in a vessel of the Royal Navy, HMS *Kent*. Modifications had been carried out to the aeroplane's interior which had new furnishings to provide two state rooms, one for Prince Edward and Prince George, and the other for their staff. The take off was made on Monday, April 27 at 2.44 pm and the three and a half hour journey to Le Bourget begun. In the event, it was not among the most comfortable of journeys that the passengers had enjoyed and it was not until 6.10 pm that landfall was made, so that it is hardly surprising that the following day was spent in some relaxations which included a visit to Paris.

The Wednesday following saw the continuation of the homeward journey and, during this, escort was provided by two RAF flying boats. The weather throughout was, although calm, otherwise poor, and visibility was restricted. It had never been the Prince of Wales' method to remain long in the cabin during a journey by air and this was no exception, since before long Captain Olley found him on the flight-deck. As it happened this enabled him to demonstrate to his passenger the fact that radio was being used to establish the position of the aircraft which was constantly in touch with the control tower at Croydon.

Indeed, while this was going on, an increasingly large crowd had begun to gather there, the London airport of the day, since it was believed that the Argosy would land there and the princes would complete their journey by car. In fact there had never been any intention to do so and the liner crossed the coast near to Dungeness and followed a route along the Edenbridge valley, passed over Dorking and headed for Windsor.

At just after 1 pm Captain Olley circled Windsor Great Park and slowly brought the big biplane in to land on Smith's Lawn where, with a group of spectators, stood the Duke of York waiting to welcome his brothers home. The following day, the newspapers made much, not only of the royal return but also the manner of their coming. Those which publicly supported aviation particularly seized the opportunity to describe in greater detail the aeronautical events of the trip. There was plenty to cover. Paramount among the items was that the royal brothers had been escorted over a 500-mile trip in the Pan-American Grace Airways' tri-motor belonging to Homer Farris. These courtesies had been performed by Peruvian Army fighters from Lima, of which two had remained with the airliner as far as Ica, 200 miles south, where a further escort took over until Arequipa was reached, after a flight of four and a half hours. Other reports did not fail to emphasise the amount of personal flying that the Prince of Wales had performed in the Puss Moth aircraft, a second example of which had been borrowed for the use of the Duke of Gloucester.

Events such as these would still be vividly in Prince Edward's mind when he paid a visit to Manchester on May 9, and this was shown when he addressed a gathering of businessmen in the Free Trade Hall three days later. He said: 'I am very interested in the development of aviation. Although not very apparent at the moment, there is undoubtedly a great future for aviation in South America . . .. With the exception of one journey, my brother and I did all our travels in the Argentine by air, and in English machines all the time. From experience I can describe Argentina as one vast aerodrome . . .. It seems to me a real opportunity for the railways, who will be confronted with competition, to anticipate that competition by

The first cabin machine owned by the Prince of Wales, DH80A Puss Moth, G-ABBS (c/n 2020).

A close-up of the foreward section of G-ABEG. The Cadwallader red dragon badge was later to be worn by the present Prince of Wales on his flying overalls.

initiating some form of air service in co-operation with the railway system'.

In the light of the fact that, with the Duke of Gloucester in a second machine, the Prince had arrived from Hendon at Manchester's Barton Aerodrome in his own Puss Moth; and that the address to the Birmingham Chamber of Commerce on the previous day had been couched in similar terms; there were those among his listeners who recalled a speech by his father when Prince of Wales at London's Guildhall in 1901 which had concluded with the exhortation: 'Wake up, England!'

The Puss Moth that was being so hard worked in 1931 was G-ABNN. This was to set the fashion for royal aircraft for some time to come since the doubled final pair of registration letters was to be repeated as a mark of royal ownership as new machines were acquired. It was about this time that it was realised that if a larger machine was added to the unofficially-termed 'Royal Flight' a greater flexibility would result and this resulted in the first use of a three-engined Westland Wessex monoplane for the opening of Roborough airport in July. In fact this was no sudden decision, for the Prince of Wales had paid a special visit to the works at Yeovil during 1930 to make an inspection of the prototype.

The same Wessex, G-ABEG, was loaned to the Prince for his tour of France and subsequent holiday at Cannes between August 18 and September 19 when the pilot was still the redoubtable Flight Lieutenant Fielden. He worked with Mr T. Jenkin, the ground engineer, and these two men were to be jointly responsible for royal aeroplanes for more than a decade.

Meanwhile the other members of the Royal Family were in no way losing their interest in aviation since all the royal brothers were now qualified pilots and, as might be expected, the Duke of York was to be frequently seen at his public duties in the uniform of his chosen Service. As, for example, his attendance at the Royal Tournament at Olympia, together with the Duchess and their five-year-old daughter, now Her Majesty the Queen, who is on record as having returned the compliments of the guard of honour with a smart salute delivered bare-headed and with the wrong hand!

The Spacious Firmament

'The spacious firmament on high,
With all the blue etherial sky'
Joseph Addison

Prince Edward's royal duties in no way diminished in 1932 but it seemed that he was able to cover a vast number of calls on his time because of his continued use of aircraft to get about, 'as confidently and unhesitatingly as other people take to their cars' as one correspondent put it. In fact, a small change in the pattern had taken place for it seemed that the Prince was using his personal aircraft to a more marked extent although he still flew in Service machines from time to time as witness his experience in flying off an aircraft carrier during George V's Review of the Fleet.

The wide variety of uses to which aeroplanes might be put by a busy Prince was demonstrated as early as February when the Puss Moth had flown its owner to a couple of hunt meets, the first on the 15th when riding with the Quorn and the second, 11 days later, when attending a meeting of the Grafton Hounds. While later the same month it was by air that the Prince had journeyed to Bordon Camp where, as Colonel-in-Chief of the Royal Scots Fusiliers, he was to bid farewell to the 1st Battalion that was about to depart for Palestine.

However, for official occasions abroad Service machines from No 24 Squadron were still used. One such in 1932 was when a Fairey IIIF took the Prince from Northolt to Le Bourget on May 12 in order that he might attend the funeral of President Doumer, who had died in a hail of bullets from a mad assassin at an ex-servicemen's exhibition in Paris, six days before.

The same type of aircraft were to carry aloft both Prince Edward and Prince George when the two circled in separate machines over the assembled Fleet off Spithead the following July, following a demonstration which included the bombing of targets towed behind destroyers by machines of the Fleet Air Arm, watched from HMS *Courageous* by their Royal Highnesses in the company of their father. Now, as the two droned above the vessels, the order was given to the Fleet; 'Stand by to receive a message from His Majesty the King'. Then Prince Edward used the radio telephone of the Fairey IIIF in which he was flying to deliver King George's words: 'In the name of the King . . . It gives me great pleasure to inspect the ships' companies I saw aboard the Fleet Flagship this morning. I am now enjoying watching the operations of the carriers'.

It was three days later that the technical press appeared with a rash of pictures showing a diminutive high-wing monoplane racer that had distinguished itself in the King's Cup Air Race a little earlier. This was the Comper Swift and an example fitted with a de Havilland Gipsy III engine, one of three thus equipped with the four cylinder in-line 120 hp motor to give a still higher performance, had been entered by the Prince. The pilot was naturally Edward Fielden and as it taxied out to the starting point the £550 racer with its entry number '52' boldly displayed on a white disc across the fin and rudder left no doubt as to its source as it was finished in the blue and red of the Brigade of Guards.

The total distance of the course was 1,223 miles from Brooklands on a circular route via Northampton, Ipswich, Desford, Woodford, Hooton Park, Birmingham, Whitchurch, Portsmouth, Shoreham and Abingdon, and in a field of 42 starters the competition was fierce. Even so, although first place was secured by W.L. Hope, Edward Fielden, the quiet man who flew in a rumpled lounge suit and striped scarf, managed to bring the Comper CLA7, G-ABWW, to second at 155.75 mph.

The following month Princes George and Edward were once more due to resume their official duties abroad, for England was at that time the possessor of a vast-flung empire which had to enjoy the connecting links with the Mother Country which only visits by the Royal Family could forge. Both young men had left England in separate private machines with a third acting as escort, and their first destination was Le Bourget. From here they boarded the Simplon Express which was to take them to Venice. A Short Kent flying boat, the *Satyrus* of Imperial Airways, picked them up from the Italian port and flew them to Corfu where the Flagship of the Mediterranean Fleet, HMS *Queen Elizabeth*, was waiting.

Both Princes remained on board for three days before embarking on the carrier HMS *Glorious* on August 16 and it was from this vessel that they flew once more in Fairey IIIF machines. Hardly were they in the air than an unexpected fog descended and it was only by the greatest of good luck that the pilot of the machine with the Prince of Wales on board was able to make his way back to the ship and carry out an uneventful landing. Not so, the Duke of Gloucester, who had to endure the discomforts of sitting 'blind' in a cramped cockpit while the pilot circled in the gloom until the fog had thinned sufficiently for a safe landing on the carrier to be attempted.

September found the royal brothers at home once more but not for long as the beginning of the month saw fresh calls on the Prince of Wales' time when he accepted an invitation to open the Anglo-Danish Exhibition at Copenhagen. The trip began at the Prince's home at Sunningdale and a three-engined Spartan Cruiser monoplane was used to take him to Croydon Aerodrome, once the Waddon training station where both he and his brother, the Duke of Kent, had received their early pilot training, but now reconstructed and enlarged since 1929 to be the new airport of London in succession to Hounslow.

Here he had transferred to *Hercules* G-AAXC—the last word in luxury airliners of the day and the type that gave its name to a whole class of large, comfortable machines that plied the regular services of Imperial Airways. Although this was the first trip the Prince had made in a Handley Page machine since the memorable flight in 1919 it was by no means his first visit to Croydon since its alterations for, as an enthusiastic air traveller even three years before, he had visited the aerodrome on March 26 1929 in an earlier biplane of Imperial Airways, *Argosy* G-EBLO, 'City of Birmingham', such as had brought him to Smith's Lawn at Windsor on another occasion.

On this journey September 2 had proved to have poor weather prospects and departure was delayed so that the eventual arrival at Schipol was delayed by 40 minutes, and this in turn prevented the final touch-down at Kastrup, the airport of the Danish capital, until the evening. Six days later the Prince once again seized a fresh opportunity to widen his air experience for he managed to fly across Denmark in a seaplane, this time of the Royal Danish Naval Air Arm with Lieutenant Harms at the controls. After his stay in this Scandinavian country was over, the Prince of Wales was able to accept an invitation to visit another so that October saw him in Sweden. It was here that the Aero-transport Company placed in his hands both a Junkers Ju 52/3m together with the services of Captain Ernst Roll and, in the German tri-motor further hours were logged.

The year was drawing towards its close when the Prince returned to England and now, he decided, was the time to review the position with regard to the machines that were suitable for his work and indeed formed the nucleus of the specialised Flight that he was to bring into being at a later day. In order to make the best decisions he consulted Flight Lieutenant Fielden on all aspects of the matter and the two arrived at some decisions that were to mean several changes in the Flight at Hendon.

One of the most difficult solutions to arrive at was the fate of the pair of Gipsy Moths, but these it was decided to retain, although relegated purely to a sporting role. The Puss Moth, on the other hand, although a useful machine, had its limitations since it had been designed as a two or three-seater so that it was cramped if any baggage had to be taken and, should the assistance of either an ADC or a valet be required for perhaps even an overnight stay, the problem always presented itself, which was to be taken by air, the cases or the staff?

In the light of this dilemma a look was taken at what British aircraft manufacturers had to offer in much the same class and a solution to the problem seemed to be available in a new design that had only appeared on the market earlier the same year. This was the de Havilland DH83, known as the Fox Moth, which had, for a sacrifice of some ten miles an hour off the top speed, compared with the earlier type, the advantage of accommodation for four persons.

Adding that the proposed new design still gave a useful cruising speed of nearly 95 mph, Fielden presented the facts to the Prince and in consequence it was decided to dispose of the earlier type. The last flight in it was made on the occasion of the Prince's visit to Oldstock School when he flew from Sunningdale to Longford Castle, Salisbury, and the address which he delivered to the assembled boys was enhanced a hundred-fold by the knowledge that their golden-haired hero had arrived in such a manner.

Shortly before Christmas 1932 the new machine arrived in the form of Fox Moth G-ACDD finished, like its predecessors, in the Brigade of Guards colours. The slight reduction in speed was obviously brought about by the uncommon arrangement of

G-ACDD, the DH83 Fox Moth (c/n 4033) used by Prince Edward at the end of 1932. The Guards colour scheme is applied to the fin and rudder in a slightly different manner from that of the Puss Moth.

the passenger quarters which were within a small, enclosed cabin. The pilot sat behind and above this, in an open cockpit, much after the manner of the driver of a Hansom cab.

Although the immediate requirements were met by the new acquisition it was obvious that it was in some measure only a temporary solution and a decision about the addition of a much larger aircraft to the Flight had to be taken. The usefulness of this had been proven by the use of the Wessex and by the machines chartered from Imperial Airways. The advice of Edward Fielden was that a proven design should be chosen and the use by Australian Airways of the Vickers Viastra seemed testimony enough. Consequently an order was placed for one of the type at a cost of £4,250 on November 3 1932.

This was to be a special model of the type, the first time that a custom-built aircraft had been constructed for a member of the royal family and in this connection a twin-engined version was required, a point that had to be stated since the Viastra had been designed with both single and twin-engined variants.

The royal, two-motor version was designated the Vickers Type 259, or Viastra Mk X, and construction began at Woolston, the former Supermarine works now taken over by Vickers. The historic nature of the order they had received was not lost on the company and with pardonable pride they published details of the fittings and modifications that were incorporated in G-ACCC.

The furnishings were carried out in a variety of Empire wood veneers and the side panels were lined with chamois leather where they came into contact with the bearers, cut from balsa wood to prevent their acting as sound boards. Sound-proofing was achieved by insulating the cabin walls with acoustic blankets and Hairlok while the whole was further lined by fireproof paper or fibre. Double glazing was fitted to the windows.

All the special items, it was declared, had been produced and designed in the works, except for the cigarette lighters, and priority had been given to taking as great advantage as possible of the space available and of providing a high degree of comfort, a contribution no doubt, thought especially desirable from the fact that the normal range of 700 miles could be increased by the extra fuel tank under the fuselage. The result, stated the builders, was a machine 'as comfortable as possible for long journeys', with 'a cabin quieter than an express train'. Publicity apart, there is no denying that the Viastra was a very useful machine with a good turn of speed, some 130 mph, for what, with a wing span of 70 feet, was a relatively large aeroplane by the standards of the day.

This was the fourth aircraft that the Prince of Wales owned, all having been paid for out of his personal capital, not public funds, and on May 16 1933 the new machine was granted a Certificate of Airworthiness. The same day Flight Lieutenant Fielden took Prince Edward from the royal landing ground at Windsor to Cardiff and then back to Hendon where the Esher Trophy was to be presented to No 604 (County of Middlesex) Squadron of the Auxiliary Air Force. All the components of the R(Aux)AF were at that time still considered to be light-bomber squadrons and it was not to be until July 23 1934 that this particular one was to assume the fighter role. The reason why the Prince was to

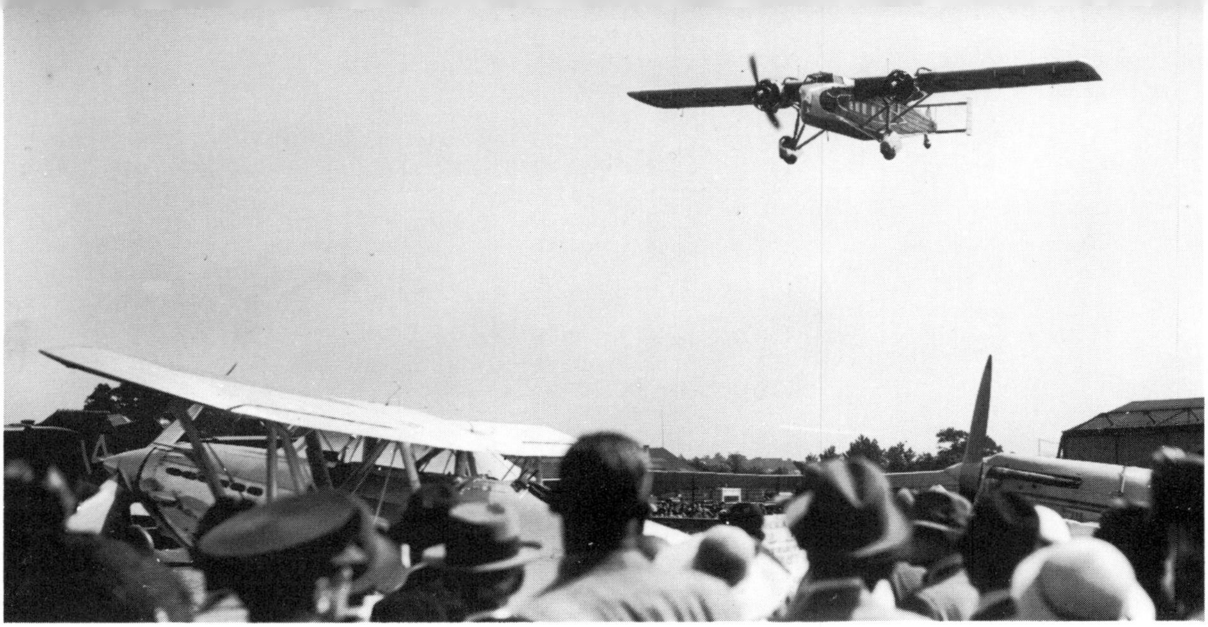

The Vickers Viastra Mk X G-ACCC, with the Prince of Wales aboard, lands at Hendon in 1934 over the Prototype Supermarine F7/30 and Hawker Fury biplane ('Flight International').

carry out this particular duty in his new aeroplane was by virtue of his holding the rank of Honorary Air-Commodore-in-Chief of the Auxiliary Service.

On May 20 the Viastra once more came in for critical inspection by informed eyes for it was used to fly the Prince to the second civil air display organised by the Guild of Air Pilots and Air Navigators of the British Empire where several hundred of its members were gathered.

The position with regard to the equipment of the 'Royal Flight'—title still quite unofficial—was not entirely new since it consisted of four machines, all finished in the colours of the Brigade of Guards, which had tended to become a tradition, although the arrangement of the shades and the application of the trim varied from machine to machine in order to do artistic and aesthetic justice to the appearance.

The latest among the changes had been suggested in February, when the possibility of obtaining one of the new de Havilland Dragons had been looked into and it was even considered at one point that the freshly-acquired Viastra might want replacement before long. However, this proposal was not followed up in quite that manner and the Vickers aircraft was still in service, although used decreasingly, when one of the new biplanes was delivered. This was G-ACGG, finished like the others in red, blue and silver, which was flown in to Hendon on June 12 1933.

The manner whereby this aircraft was procured is of interest since the original proposal was that an exchange be effected for the Fox Moth, Puss Moth and Gipsy Moth already owned by the Prince. However, it was pointed out that the value of these three second-hand biplanes did not equal that of the new de Havilland and so an agreement was made whereby the three be taken in payment for a basic de Havilland Dragon and the furnishings be provided at cost. Thus it was that, nine days after delivery, it was in a biplane once more that the Prince of Wales paid a visit to Mousehold Aerodrome, the same Norwich venue which he had visited five years previously in the historic Bristol F2B.

Although seen less frequently in the air after this, the Viastra was not entirely neglected and it was to assist in the flying of this that a second pilot was sometimes taken, in the shape of Flight Lieutenant H.M. Mellor, who, more used to Service aircraft, must have appreciated such refinements as the Vickers had to offer like the KLM type drift indicator, the red warning light that indicated the cabin door was still to be locked before take off and the luminous dials in the instrument panel, which was also illuminated for day use.

It was with the two pilots aboard that the Viastra was the victim of a strange event on March 9 1934 that was to have echoes 26 years later involving the Prince's niece. Prince Edward was in the process of being taken home to Hendon in mid-afternoon and he was accompanied by Admiral Halsey from Hilsea, Portsmouth. Just as the royal machine was near to Hindhead a flight of Hawker Harts was seen approaching from the south at some 2,500 feet. Hardly had Fielden looked at his watch and noted that it indicated 3.10 pm when another RAF

Once more in the Brigade of Guards colours, DH84 Dragon purchased by the Prince of Wales in the summer of 1933.

machine was observed to be approaching, this time a Bristol Bulldog fighter in the colours of 'A' Flight of No 111 Squadron. But the newcomer was on a north-west course and at much the same altitude as the Harts. The latter flew over the Viastra some distance aft, harmlessly enough, but the fighter banked to port and with a separation of only about 200 yards passed the royal machine in the opposite direction before seeming to disappear.

Another member of the flight crew was the ground engineer, Mr T. Jenkins who chose this moment to inspect the motor and tail surfaces on that side through the cabin door. He was astonished to see that they had gained an unofficial escort flying very close in the form of a Bulldog machine. Just in case the procedure was in order and he had not been informed he then went to the other side, half expecting to find another fighter there. There was none. Perplexed for a moment he paused on that side just long enough to see what he thought for a moment was the expected machine slide into view, but no, this was the first fighter (for he had already noted the serial number) and there it was before his eyes again, standing out bold and black against the immaculate silver finish, K2221.

On first spotting the intruder he had made vigorous signs to the pilot of the single-seater to keep away and he waved his arms again now. The pilot seemed to take this for a sign of welcome and moved his machine to fly abreast of the Viastra, so that it was not visible to the two officers on the flight deck. More hand signals had no effect and for fully two minutes the strange fighter kept company with G-ACCC only about 50 feet from the wing tip. Then, just as suddenly as it had appeared, the Bulldog vanished. With a jerk the nose came up, the pilot flung it into a bank over the top of the royal aircraft, clearing the tip by only some 30 feet, and it was gone. Quite obviously something had to be done about this state of affairs and Edward Fielden had to lodge an official report in which he stated that, had the final manoeuvre been made below the Viastra rather than above, the trailing aerial would have been carried away.

Was it high spirits that caused the fighter pilot to behave in this manner, misinterpretation of the signals or a genuine belief that the large machine was in some way acting as an exercise target? The answer will never be known; but it is sufficient to say that the reply to the official complaint that Fielden lodged brought from the Director of Training, Air Commodore C.L. Countney, CB, CBE, DSO, a firm assurance that the officer in charge of the Bulldog had been given due cause to remember the cross examination which was a result of such dangerous conduct and that there was unlikely to be a repetition of the series of events.

By this time, Flight Lieutenant Fielden had received promotion by the Prince to a new and unique position for, although he still held the same rank as an officer on the reserve, it had been announced in October 1933 that he had been appointed to the position of Chief Air Pilot—the term sounds somewhat archaic today—and Extra Equerry.

Just before this, the Viastra had received what was probably its most intense period of use except for that which took place at a later date in its career during Air Ministry trials in connection with radio

direction finding, since the late summer of 1933 had found it employed for several trips to and from the Continent. It was during one of these, on a return flight from Paris on August 15, that it was forced down by bad weather at South Nutfield in Surrey and some damage was sustained. The Prince was not aboard at the time but a ground engineer and an RAF officer were being carried instead. It became essential that the machine be repaired as soon as possible and in consequence, poor weather or not, Vickers sent a team of men from Brooklands who worked with the aid of lamps throughout the short summer night to render the monoplane air-worthy. Once this was done it was flown straight to Eastleigh, Southampton, the next day where it was given a thorough examination before being sent to rejoin the royal machines at Hendon.

Perhaps the most memorable use of the big Viastra X, at least as far as a vast number of people were concerned, took place, however, during the summer of 1934. By now the RAF Display at Hendon—the term 'Pageant' had been dropped—had become something of a public institution and this year was no exception. An emphasis was to be noticed on some important changes, however, and these may be summed up by the statement that those items in the programme that had little military significance were now conspicuous by their absence, since the Air Estimates for that year had provided for six new squadrons. The International Disarmament Conference at Geneva, so long looked forward to as a beacon of hope by those who remembered the horrors of the First World War, had failed, and ignominiously so, and Germany, with a tightening grip of Nazism about her throat after the success of the Reichstag fire the year before, had withdrawn from the League of Nations.

Perhaps it was an appreciation of the way that international affairs were drifting that influenced those highly placed in the aircraft industry to back a seeming increase in the number of private ventures at Hendon that year. On that golden Saturday in a summer when even the reservoirs dried up, the royal Viastra, on the last trip it was to make with the Prince of Wales aboard, came in to land over a line-up of such machines in the New Types Park as the Hawker Fury, the Handley Page Heyford bomber and a strange monoplane with inverted gull wings from Supermarine. They called it the F7/30 although there were those who said it was to be called Spitfire, the first use of the name and applied to the precursor of the prototype of the subsequent bearer of the name. This, and all the types termed in the programme 'Experimental Aircraft', were inspected by the Prince who was accompanied by the Air Minister, Lord Londonderry, but it was the manner of the royal arrival that most of all impressed the crowd. 'A distinctly new note was struck', commented *Flight.*

This event apart, the next use of the aeroplane to really catch the public's attention was not to take place until October and was signalled by the preparations for the race from England to Australia in a competition for the MacRobertson Trophy. The air of excitement that occurrences such as these engendered in the public mind is impossible to define accurately today, but those who can recall the feelings at the time of man's first landing on the surface of the moon, had it taken place in a world bereft of television and where only a proportion of the population had radio, will have some idea of the feelings comon at the time.

For this competition the de Havilland organisation had produced a new and special design known as the DH88 or Comet, a sleek, almost futuristic monoplane built smoothly of wood in an age when the biplane still reigned almost supreme. Those who commented wryly that it looked almost lethal were proved not far from wrong in after years when the lessons learned in the production of the type were applied to the Mosquito, the 'wooden wonder' of the war years that were to come.

Three of these machines had been built and, in company with the 17 other starters' aircraft (all that were left from the original list of 64 hopeful entrants) were inspected by their Majesties King George and Queen Mary, together with the Prince of Wales, all of whom had travelled specially to the starting point at Mildenhall in Suffolk on the eve of the race. Perhaps it was royal pride in the country which he ruled, and perhaps the same spirit infused the press photographers present; but it must be more than coincidence that the cameras clicked most furiously when the Prince stopped to talk to Comet entrants C.W.A. Scott and Tom Campbell Black. Their aircraft, *Grosvenor House,* was destined to win first place in the contest. The cameramen also went into a flurry of activity when the King and Queen paused before Jim and Amy Morrison's similar *Black Magic*.

The race was, in fact, the culmination of what in retrospect was to seem a vintage year for the association of the Royal Family with aviation, as it had seen the establishment of a new institution of the air. In the days when the sun had not yet set on the British Empire in its old form and when the term 'Commonwealth' was a reference to a long-past event in the history books, there used to be celebrated annually an Empire Day. It was the germ of this idea that was taken by the Air League who had the concept of linking it with aviation.

Up and down the country on the appointed day both civil and Service aerodromes were thrown open to the public and to one of the latter, Bircham Newton, came the King and Queen, thus making history by the fact that this was the first occasion since the war years that they had visited an RAF Station. This was not all, for the commander was none other than Wing Commander Ray Collishaw whom the King had previously met when the two had walked side by side down the line of Sopwith Camels flanked by their Flight Commanders at Le Nieppe in August 1918 when the Canadian officer, then a Major, was in command of No 203 Squadron in France. Now, 16 years later they were doing much the same thing but there were also civilians present, this time including Sir Philip Sassoon and Lord Londonderry, Queen Mary who, perhaps with a mother's pride, was noticed by some taking a more protracted glance than was her habit at a parked Saro Cloud similar to that in which her eldest son had journeyed to Calshot four years before.

In the flying display that followed the representative display of service machines performed in the Norfolk sky against a background of perfect weather conditions, but there were those who noted that the King, on a day when the airmen were in Service Jackets, wore an overcoat. Some added that to watch the demonstration he seemed to sit with something less than his accustomed erectness beside his wife on the bright floral arm chairs provided. Even so, for the monarch who had continued the interest in flying that his illustrious father had established, the day was a happy one as reflected in the telegram that Air Marshal Brook-Popham was later to receive from His Majesty expressing his gratitude for the organisation of the day at Bircham Newton. In the matter of telegrams the King had no monopoly for the historic first Empire Air Day saw both the Prince of Wales and the Prime Minister send their congratulations to the organisers.

Meanwhile, it would be wrong to conclude that the interest in aviation shown by the other young men of the royal family was any less keen and it is not necessary to look far through the flying journals of the time to find proof of this. Typical was the summer of 1934 when Prince George, the Duke of Kent, attended the meeting of the Royal Air Force Flying Club. Previously this organisation had

Above left *Flight Lieutenant Edward Hedley Fielden at the door of his caravan at the time of the 1934 King's Cup Air Race* ('Flight International').

Right *The Prince of Wales with Lindsay Everard MP and Lieutenant Commander Harold E. Perrin, Secretary of the Royal Aero Club, talk to the winners of the 1934 England-Australia Air Race, Tom Campbell Black and C.W.A. Scott, in front of their DH88 Comet* Grosvenor House ('Flight International').

confined its membership to those whose names appeared on the Reserve List but the scope was now widened so that past and present Service members of all the flying services became eligible, including the RNAS, RFC and the University Air Squadrons. The result was a greatly widened spectrum of possible membership and it was in effect to mark this that so many notable persons attended the 1934 meeting.

Included among these were Sir John Salmond, Major H. Butler and Lieutenant Colonel Shelmerdine, Director of Civil Aviation, in company with the President of the Club, Lord Trenchard. That his Lordship enjoyed this position was, of course, entirely right and proper for here was the man who had done almost more than any other officer to establish the Royal Air Force as a separate fighting Service.

Very probably this was unknown to the group which awaited the arrival of the Duke of Kent on the fine Saturday afternoon. The aircraft bearing the Prince punctually arrived at 4 pm from the direction of Reading. Its appearance triggered off much interest, not only from the fact that here was one of the first uses of the Prince of Wales' new de Havilland DH84, but also from the fact that here, to be readily seen by all, was an illustration of the faith that the Royal Family had in aviation and the determination of all its members to encourage the use of aeroplanes. At this point in time it would be an almost impossible task for any historian to calculate the benefits that civil aviation in Great Britain gained from this, but there is no question that those from the publicity value alone were enormous since the aircraft were always up to date and represented the cream of what was then the foremost aviation industry in the world in the best light since the machines used for royal journeys

Above *Escorted by Wing Commander Raymond Collishaw on his left, King George V inspects RAF Bircham Newton in May 1935* (Canadian Public Archives).

Left *Wing Commander Collishaw, George V, Lord Londonderry and Queen Mary watch the air display at Bircham Newton on May 24 1935* (Planet News).

were never of foreign manufacture. '. . . the Prince must have made thousands of converts to the cause of air travel', said *Flight*.

The business of 'conversion' was to be continued, this time personally by King George's eldest son, on the occasion of opening the present building of the Royal Air Force College at Cranwell, before the vintage year of 1934 was out. From the time it had been opened on February 5 1920, the former HMS *Daedelus* where Prince Albert had briefly served had made do with the hutted accommodation of the war years. The greater part of this had now been swept away in a great reconstruction programme. To open officially the new buildings the Prince of Wales would not have considered using any other form of transport than air and thus it was that the Dragon G-ACGG set down His Royal Highness, appropriately wearing the uniform of an Air Marshal, to be greeted by the Air Minister, Lord Londonderry, the AOC Cranwell, Air Vice-Marshal G.S. Mitchell and the Lord Lieutenant of Lincolnshire, Lord Yarborough. The group then proceeded to the main building, which had been designed by James Grey West, OBE, and behind which lay the housing arrangements for 150 cadets divided into three wings.

At first sight it may appear that the constant changes of aircraft for royal use were no more than the actions of an irresponsible young man. However it is as true of royalty as of their subjects that anyone is at liberty to do as he likes with his own money and although there may have been self-righteous people who advocated huge donations from the Royal Family to charity instead, there is no question that these new and up-to-date machines constantly introduced gave, as a direct result, employment to many. They might otherwise have been tempted to anticipate the modern 'brain drain' by half a century. Instead they remained in the British aircraft industry dealing with the enlarging order books that the operation of the best products by royalty encouraged.

It may well be that the retention of some of our finest technicians in these islands, where they were able to make an incalculable contribution to their country's cause in the years of conflict that were looming ever nearer at this time, was in part a result of the unceasing up-grading of royal machines even as the immaculate Dragon was in use, at the Cranwell ceremonies.

Only a month before this, Flight Lieutenant Fielden had begun negotiations with the de Havilland Company for yet another modernisation of the 'Royal Flight', a title that was still strictly unofficial. Part of his duties was to keep abreast of aviation progress and it had not gone unnoticed that the company was even then beginning to supersede the DH84 with the DH89, a type later to become known in the civil field as the Dragon Rapide and, in the Service where it was to be introduced as a radio trainer and communications aircraft, as the Dominie.

Known as the Dragon Six at the time, the design was offered to the public at a basic price of £3,750 but fitting it out to the higher standards requisite for a special machine would raise the cost to £4,369 14 shillings (£4,369.70), including £10 for the paint scheme in the now traditional Brigade of Guards colours. In the light of the fact that it had been decided to replace the Viastra as well, it was finally decided to purchase two examples of the Rapide and to partially offset the cost of £8,150 by the sale of the Dragon.

Although the new pair were still to be delivered the latter type was sold on February 9 1935 to Richard Shuttleworth of Old Warden, Bedfordshire, who was even then beginning to found the collection of airworthy vintage aircraft that is now known as the Shuttleworth Trust. To digress a moment, it is interesting to note that the idea behind this purchase was to use the machine as a vehicle for the conduction of trials in illuminated aerial advertising with neon tubes. It can now only be a matter of regret that although the experiments would seem to have been crowned with success—a Rapide was a common sight over various parts of the country in the immediate post-war years calling for '2 million National Savers' from the night sky—the historic aircraft was disposed of and may not be found in the collection today.

The first of the new Rapides was delivered to Hendon in the form of G-ACTT (c/n 6257) on April 26 1935, one month ahead of schedule, although it is only fair to point out that the second machine was slightly late, not being delivered until June 8. This was G-ADDD (c/n 6283), the reason for the tight delivery schedule being that 1935 was Jubilee year when King George was to celebrate 25 years on the throne and in connection with this a heavy flying programme was anticipated.

The Silver Jubilee year was one marked by a wide variety of functions official and non-official. Students of social history may suggest that this was so because it meant relief from the years of the Depression when work was scarce, giving birth to such historic events as the Jarrow March to London. Others may state that the tide of patriotism was an expression of the genuine feeling that people held for George V who, a few years before, had nearly been unhorsed when riding in Hyde Park by a surge of his male subjects anxious to shake his hand. Again it may well have been that the age

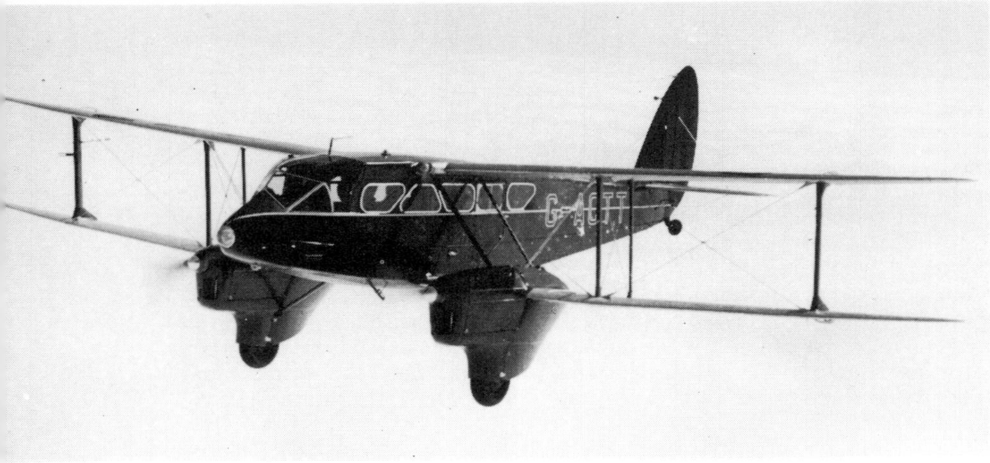

Left *The first of the Prince's DH89 Dragon Rapides, G-ACTT, acquired in April 1935* ('Flight International').

Opposite page *Air Chief Marshal the Prince of Wales, King George V in the uniform of a Marshal of the Royal Air Force and Air Vice-Marshal the Duke of York at the time of the Silver Jubilee celebrations, 1935* (Crown Copyright).

was one when the 'stiff upper lip' traditionally associated with the Englishman went hand in hand with an ability to enjoy himself and show no embarrassment at doing so, that had not yet been eroded by pre-digested entertainment.

Probably the feelings that gave the fine, hot summer of 1935 a special atmosphere were a result of several of these factors, more than the decorated streets even in the suburbs of London, miles from the processional route to be followed for the journey to St Paul's Cathedral and the Service of Thanksgiving there; more than the decorated private cars that went about their owners' personal business bedecked with flags and streamers; more even than the popular songs rendered by every danceband, broadcasting or not, and sold in thousands as gramophone records. Of these ditties there were many. One of the most popular was called 'Gentlemen, the King!' and contained a reference to 'The Army, the Navy, the boys in the sky . . .' and for the latter the year of 1935 was an especially momentous one, for the Royal Air Force was to enjoy the privilege of its first-ever Royal Review.

Detailed planning for this had begun during the preceding year and by the early spring of the Jubilee year the final plans had been worked out. At about the same time the Duke of Gloucester was in New Zealand where he had made his own contribution to the encouragement of aviation. The main part of this work had been carried out in conjunction with the New Zealand Air Force, not yet enjoying the 'Royal' title, when the Prince had made a long flight covering many of the valleys and lakes of South Island in a type with which he was certainly familiar, a Puss Moth, then the Service's only example of the type, 2125, which had been purchased for £1,000 in August, four years before. Despite the fact that Prince Henry had completed a course of pilot training only a little later than his elder brother, the pilot on this trip was the redoubtable Flight Lieutenant Maurice W. Buckley, an early member of the old Permanent Air Force who was to rise to the rank of Air Commodore in the years to follow.

This was not the only contribution to the cause of flying which the royal brothers were to make in 1935, for a later occasion was to find the Duke and Duchess of York making use of *Draco,* a liner of the Imperial Airways fleet, as the swiftest means of travelling to Brussels.

The thoughts of the majority of people in the aviation world were, however, concentrated once more on Mildenhall where the eagerly-anticipated Royal Review was to take place on Saturday, July 6, an occasion marked by the fact that it had been announced that King George V was to wear the uniform of a Marshal of the Royal Air Force for the first time.

The squadrons chosen to represent the Service were ordered to rendezvous at the station on Monday, July 1, and the 38 units concerned were detailed to take part in full rehersals on the subsequent Tuesday and Thursday. In order to accommodate the 5,000 officers and men who had in their care the 356 aircraft, a veritable canvas town sprang up at Mildenhall and, in addition, as large an assembly as possible of the latest mechanical aids to aircraft servicing was gathered and aviation correspondents made particular mention of the Zwicky fuel bowsers. These were early examples of the refuelling tenders that were not to appear in strength until 1937, capable of taking 350 gallons of petrol and from this, replenishing the tanks of three machines

simultaneously. The Zwicky organisation built them on a variety of chassis including those of Albion, Crossley and Morris CD design.

The day of the first RAF Royal Review was marked from an early hour by bright sunshine and the procession of cars with the royal party arrived at 11 am. With King George V in the first vehicle was Queen Mary and the party included Their Royal Highnesses the Prince of Wales and the Duke of York, the two royal brothers most closely connected with Service aviation at that time. The distinguished visitors also included the Duchess of York, the Maharaja of Kashmir and Lord Trenchard. The Royal Party was joined by Air Chief Marshal Sir H. Brooke Popham, the former AOC-in-C, Air Defence of Great Britain, and sometime Wing Commander in the Royal Flying Corps with the rank of Acting Lieutenant Colonel.

The actual review took place from an open car which cruised slowly past the lines of aircraft with their crews drawn up before them behind Flight and Squadron commanders. For this the machines were formed up in a great fan of types radiating from the Royal Standard that flew at a point between the familiar two central hangars of the base, and many young men who had followed the example of the princes and become aviation enthusiasts were glad to note that the means of giving practical expression to their interests, the Auxiliary Air Force, had a place on the right of the larger part of the regular squadrons with two Coastal Defence Units.

The inspection complete, the royal party departed for Duxford, Cambridge, and at 2.25 pm the King, with his entourage, mounted the saluting base for the flypast. Until this occasion the custom of passing over a senior officer's whereabouts had been little used for ceremonial purposes although King George had experienced something similar before the outbreak of war, as detailed in an earlier chapter, the practice probably becoming more firmly established for military use by the ritual flights over the base by returning aircraft after an operational sortie in France during 1914-1918. But what was to take place now was something very different, the greatest flypast of military aircraft that the world had ever seen, no less, and a great display of aerial might. While the band of the RAF College, Cranwell, supplied background music at Mildenhall, 162 were now to pass above the visitors' heads.

As the time crept to 2.30 pm a heavy droning filled the air and, exactly on the half hour, there appeared the leaders in the form of No 99 Squadron's Handley Page Heyford bombers, supported by those of No 10 to complete the Heavy Bomber group. Two miles behind followed the Light Bombers, four squadrons of them, spread two spans between individual machines, all of the Hawker Hart type. There followed the Army Co-operation aircraft, again flying in squadrons separated by 500 yards of air space and although these presented another brave sight against the azure blue background of the summer sky, they were all similar biplane derivatives of the Light Bomber Group.

To complete Phase 1 of the Jubilee Flypast the appearance of 70 fighters drawn from ten squadrons next brought the King to the salute with the faster machines, Gloster Gauntlets and Hawker Furies, constituting the second Group, allowing the Bristol Bulldogs, 30 miles an hour slower, to go ahead.

Phase 2 of the Jubilee Review consisted entirely of a display by the Gauntlets of No 19 Squadron, the only unit to have the type for demonstration at the time, which returned to carry out a flying drill display. Phase 3 was perhaps the most impressive of all and was made up of 17 squadrons from the first part of the ceremonial, back once more having made a great circle over the countryside. Again the inescapable roar of the massed engines assaulted the ears so that the very air seemed to throb with the undulating note and at 1,200 feet 155 aircraft seemed to blacken the sky as the summer sun dipped towards the horizon. Then, 35 minutes after His Majesty had mounted the dais with its roof supports gaily wound with bunting, peace once more descended over Duxford, and in the sudden silence the spectators realised that the first Royal Review in the history of the Royal Air Force was all over.

Meanwhile it had been found that the anticipated use for the two Rapides owned by the Prince of Wales had not in fact materialised and it was decided to sell one of them. The first to be delivered was therefore disposed of on February 24 1936, the purchaser being Olley Air Services, the company established and still retaining as its Chief Pilot the same man who had captained the Argosy of Imperial Airways that had brought Prince Edward home to Smith's Lawn a few years before.

By this time, however, things had changed, Stuart Hibbert had announced on 'the wireless', as radio was usually called in those days, that 'the King's life is drawing slowly towards its close'. George V, the monarch who had seen in his reign the birth of air transport, the Royal Air Force and organised aerial warfare, died peacefully at Sandringham as the result of a chill on January 20 1936.

When Their Rage is Up

The English—when their rage is up, they will not easily be pacified for they have high and haughty stomachs'
Diary of a Tudor traveller

The rage of the English was not yet raised, at least as far as it registered on their public face in 1936 although Stanley Baldwin, the Prime Minister, had promised the country two years before, that if disarmament proved impossible, steps would be taken to strengthen the air defences and five new Flying Training Schools had been opened during 1935. But the image of England which any visitor might have gathered on the wet and sullen January day when the Bluejackets had drawn their late King through the capital to his rest at Windsor was of a mourning land at peace.

Even so, behind the public image there were changes taking place undreamed of at the previous accession. At the death of a sovereign it is necessary for an Accession Council to take place within 24 hours and Prince Edward, now King, was bothered by the wretched train service that connected Sandringham to London. It was natural that he should think of the advantages of flying and straight away he summoned Edward Fielden to his aid. It was decided that the new King should be flown to London, the first British monarch to travel by aeroplane in history. With him travelled his brother, the Duke of York, who had to leave his wife with more than the usual reluctance since she was confined to bed at the time with a severe attack of influenza that threatened to turn to pneumonia. Thus began one of the shortest reigns in English history and some were to recall in the months which followed that, during the funeral of George V, the King who had chosen not to fly but had encouraged aviation, the orb had seemed to topple for a moment on the coffin during the ceremony: while there were others who, with doubtful taste, had pointed to the forced landing the Prince of Wales had made on November 16 1929 near Woking in Surrey when the Moth had sustained a broken axle.

With the historic flight to London the reign of the new King seemed set for fresh paths of progress such as His Majesty must have had in mind when he wrote later, 'I had no desire to go down in history as Edward the Reformer. Edward the Innovator—that might have been more to the point'. One of the first innovations was the acquisition of an official aeroplane to be paid for from Air Ministry funds and the search for a suitable machine to replace the single Rapide for royal duties began. At one time even an American type was considered in the form of a Lockheed Super Electra.

More immediate, and in many ways more radical, was the announcement that Flight Lieutenant Edward Hedley Fielden, AFC, was to be promoted to the rank of Wing Commander and, with effect from July 21 1936, would assume the duty of an Equerry in Waiting attached to the Royal Mews at Buckingham Palace and perform the entirely new duties of a Captain of the newly-created King's Flight. The justification of this was obvious from the increased use of the Rapide not only by the new King but by his brothers to expedite their official duties. The same year, Fielden at the centre of what was to later be termed 'the most radical innovation in the composition of the Royal Household' was created an MVO and his salary, formerly paid by the Prince through the Keeper of the Privy Purse, was now found by the RAF who also granted to ground engineers R.T. Hussey and T. Jenkins, Service equivalent NCO rank. In addition, the maintenance costs of G-ADDD were met by the Air Ministry from April 1 1936.

An examination of the amount of use to which the single Rapide was put is seen from the 61 flights that were made that year. Twelve of these were to convey King Edward VIII, now a Marshal of the Royal Air Force, eight for the Duke of Kent, five to carry the Duke of York and one at the service of the Duke of Gloucester. Perhaps the heaviest day was July 8 1936 when the King, in the company of the Duke of York and the Chief of Air Staff, had visited a number of RAF stations. The first of these was

Northolt where Nos 1 and 111 Squadrons presented a display in conjunction with visiting No 19 Squadron. The next call was on No 11 FTS at Wittering before flying to Mildenhall where Nos 38, 99 and 40 Squadrons were based. The tour was concluded at the experimental station of Martlesham Heath where there were two revolutionary fighters to be seen. One had elliptical wings and was called a Spitfire while the other was described as the Hawker F36/34 although an unofficial ceremony the same day had seen it named Hurricane.

Mindful of the increased use to which the new King was obviously going to put his aircraft, the search for a suitable replacement for the Rapide was stepped up, a responsibility that fell to Fielden in addition to his flying and command duties. That the net was cast widely in the search for recommendations that might be made to the King is shown by the inclusion of the forerunner of the Blenheim bomber, the Bristol 143, and the large Bristol Bombay on the list.

Then, quite suddenly it seemed to the public, His Majesty King Edward VIII abdicated and the Duke of York ascended the throne, creating his brother Duke of Windsor. When the latter sailed from Portsmouth for France in the destroyer *Fury* on the night of December 11, among the personal property that he left behind was the DH89 at Hendon with a total flying time of 194 hours to its credit.

One of the first announcements by King George VI, as the former Duke of York had now become, was that the King's Flight continue to exist under the captainship of Wing Commander Fielden and consequently the hunt for a new machine was to continue. Towards this aim a trial flight was arranged for March 3 1937 in the Envoy type, the product of a relatively new firm called Airspeed of Christchurch, Hants. The resultant report stated that the type was suitable, although rather small, and this lack of space was the main topic of discussion between the captain and the joint managing directors of the company, N.S. Norway, later better-known as Nevil Shute, the author, and A. Hessell Tiltman. As a result, a number of modifications were agreed on and Specification 6/37 written around them. They included provision for a radio operator and his instrument, achieved by moving the bulkhead nine inches to the rear behind the flight deck, fitting additional fuel tanks and the provision of Fairey Reed metal airscrews—while an item necessary but outside the scope of the Specification was the installation of a cocktail cabinet.

Following a series of trial flights at Martlesham Heath, the first taking place on April 21, the type was finally handed over on May 3 and it briefly flew without its allocated civil registration, G-AEXX. Once this was applied to the familiar Brigade of Guards finish there were steps to re-mark the machine with a Service serial and to put the Service engineers into uniform. Both these measures Fielden managed to postpone and it was not until after the outbreak of war when the Envoy III was handed over to No 24 Squadron's 'A' Flight at Hendon for the use of the AOC Balloon Command, Air Vice-Marshal O.T. Boyd, that it was finally marked L7270.

Meanwhile, the month before the Envoy had joined the Flight, the former King's Rapide had been sold on his behalf to Western Airways Ltd of Weston-super-Mare for the relatively good sum of £3,445.

The new, and only King's Flight machine, was immediately pressed into service, a large part of the work entailing visits to the aircraft industry now working at an increased tempo to meet orders in connection with the Expansion Scheme as well as training establishments such as that at Cranwell which the King visited once more on January 26 1938 to see the work of the Electrical and Wireless School. At much the same time countries abroad were beginning to copy the British example of using the air as a means of travel for their monarchs for, less than four months later on April 7, King Ghazi

Airspeed Envoy III showing its traditional Brigade of Guards colour scheme. Small changes took place in this during its period of use.

Farewells are said to George VI after his visit to Cranwell in 1938 before he boards the royal Airspeed Envoy for the flight home (Crown Copyright).

acquired a Percival Q6 in a flame and yellow finish, registered YI-RQH, to tour his Kingdom of Iraq.

Tentative plans were afoot before 1939 to replace the single Airspeed Envoy of the King's Flight by a more modern machine, but the outbreak of war brought these to nought and, instead, attention was diverted to providing a more military aircraft for the royal use. Perhaps the beginnings of the line of thought that materialised in the form of an American choice had been begun during the search for a Rapide replacement, for there were many raised eyebrows when an adaptation of the Super Electra airliner joined the King's Flight at Hendon via No 24 (Communications) Squadron in the form of a Lockheed Hudson, on February 12 1939.

The surprise that this choice brought about must be seen in the light of the fact that feelings were running high at this time concerning the order of 200 such machines by the British Purchasing Commission in 1938. This particular aircraft does, however, remain something of a mystery for although its Service serial N7364 is known, little else is and it seems to have languished at Hendon in company with the much-used Envoy until March 3 1940, when it passed to Heston's Photographic Development Unit.

Long before this, in fact on August 4 1939, another Hudson had joined the King's Flight in the form of N7263 direct from the assembly depot at Speke and immediate steps were taken at Farnborough to convert it for royal use. These consisted of upholstering and sound-proofing the interior and fitting six parachute chairs, while the bomb bay was altered to serve as a luggage compartment. To extend the range, extra tanks were fitted and, more as a security cover than anything else, it was referred to as a Hudson (Long Range) after the outbreak of hostilities.

The changes that war brought to the royal unit were many and must have made the days of the Coronation year display at Hendon (when the first King to be a qualified pilot in the RAF had paid a visit with his wife and two of his brothers) seem very far off; while the same may be said of the ancient Valentia biplanes used as flying classrooms that His Majesty had inspected at Cranwell. Yet the largest change was to be found in provision for gunners on the Flight staff and Sergeant H.R. Figg and AC1 L.G.A. Reed, who were posted to the unit at Benson, to which it had been moved on the outbreak of war, were unique in being the only wireless operator/air gunners ever to serve with the Flight, just as the Hudsons were the only royal machines ever to be armed.

One of the first acts of the King when war had been declared was to send a message to the RAF on Monday, September 4 and, not long after, he had paid a visit to Fighter Command. At the end of the year he had sailed to France under an escort and had visited all the Services including the RAF at a Stores Park of which both he and the Duke of Gloucester had laughed with his men at the many home comforts provided for a pet Dachshund—including even a miniature lamp-post!

In the bitter January of 1940, King George VI was back among his men in France once more, and wearing the uniform of his RAF, before beginning a round of visits to the aircraft industry the following

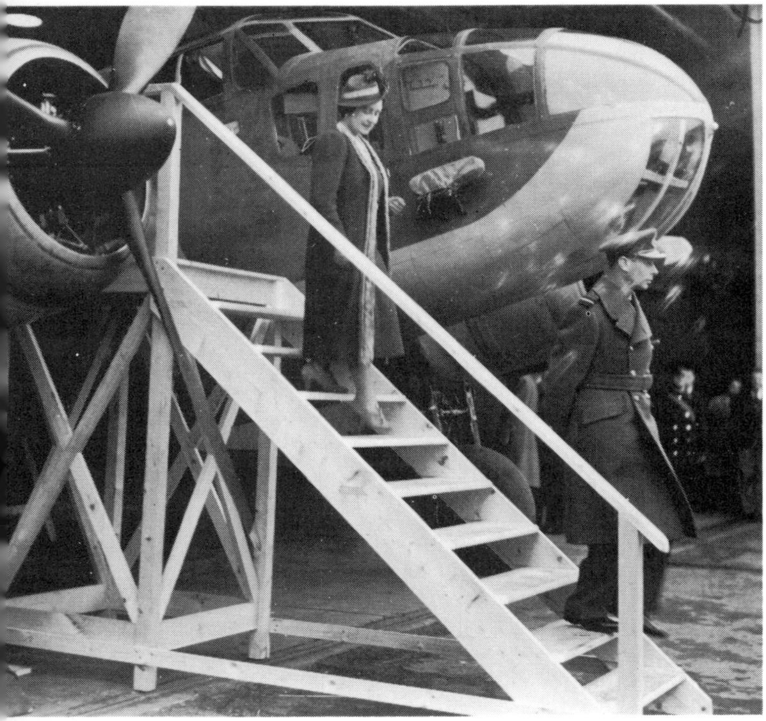

month. These included an inspection of the Bristol Aircraft Company's works at Filton where he and the Queen (now the Queen Mother) had been guided on the tour by the chief test pilot, Captain Cyril F. Uwins, and the Westland Aircraft Company at Yeovil had also been visited among others at a later date. On this particular occasion the King was wearing Army uniform since the main Westland product was the Lysander at that period, an Army Co-operation machine.

At about this time two other machines had joined the Flight at Benson. The first of these had done so on a temporary basis since it was a standard Hudson transport sent to act as a stand-by while the regular machine was unserviceable; the other, more permanent, was added on March 15 1940 in the shape of Percival Q6 P5634 from the Station Flight, Northolt, used by Air Marshal C.F.A. Portal, the newly-appointed AOC-in-C, Bomber Command.

The interest of the Royal Family in aviation continued unsparingly and, at the end of April, it was announced that the Duke of Kent had relinquished his rank of Air Vice-Mashal in order to perform welfare duties for the RAF as an Air Commodore.

With the Battle of Britain gaining momentum the King inspected the station where his Flight was a lodger unit to No 12 OTU, formed from Nos 52 and 63 Squadrons there, but not before he had given orders that the work of the station and the training programme was to go on without interruption, a fact that indicated Benson was no safe retreat from war but an RAF base on an operational footing. As if to prove this point, less than a month later, on the afternoon of August 13 the first attack was made. This was *Adlertag* and although the opening of the attacks that were to herald the hoped-for invasion was delayed because of the mist and drizzle in the Channel, conditions improved after lunch. Over Oxfordshire the first sign of enemy presence was a Junkers 88 diving out of the cloud and releasing three high explosive and one oil bomb. One of the former destroyed an air-raid shelter, which, luckily was empty since the 'imminent danger' warning was not sounded until afterwards. Certainly some masonry was blown on to the site of the married quarters, in use as a barrack block, and a large piece had fallen between 'C' and 'D' hangars damaging an Anson, but by and large the damage was slight.

Above left *King George VI presents the Distinguished Flying Cross to Flight Lieutenant Al Deere during an early wartime airfield investiture* (Imperial War Museum).

Left *King George VI and Queen Elizabeth visit the Filton factory of the Bristol Aeroplane Company where Beauforts were being produced in 1940* (Imperial War Museum).

Right *The Percival Q6 which was briefly in service with the King's Flight before it was disbanded* (Imperial War Museum).

Below right *DH95 Flamingo G-AGCC, which originally kept the doubled final letter custom for royal machines on its Service finish, shown here later in its short career* (Imperial War Museum).

Benson was not on the list of Luftwaffe targets for that day although Farnborough, Odiham and Rochford, all relatively close, were and it seems that the bomber in question was doing no more than selecting a secondary target when unable to find the main one.

Thursday, August 15, found the King at Hatfield, there to inspect a new royal machine, a DH95 Flamingo which was being prepared in the works. Use of the type, originally intended as a civil air liner or troop transport, had been suggested to Wing Commander Fielden by the Air Member for Research and Development, Air Chief Marshal Sir Wilfred Freeman. One of the three ordered, all VIP models, had been set aside for royal use and there had been some internal re-design with the alteration of window positions in consequence.

Although issued with serial number R2766 this machine in fact flew with civil registration G-AGCC and RAF roundels, to expedite its use in neutral air space in the event of the Royal Family having to flee. This was a matter in which His Majesty was seemingly more in touch with events than his officials who felt constrained to equip the machine with sugar bowls, cheese knives and butter dishes, total cost £2 5s 7d (£2.28), while the King, determined to remain among his people, was putting in what time he could to sharpen his aim at the butts.

The Flamingo was delivered by de Havilland's George Gibbins and C. Martin Sharp on September 7, while an air raid was actually taking place on London, and a course was set low over the Chilterns until it was set down at Benson to join the Hudson and Q6, the three representing the King's Flight at its optimum war strength. In fact this machine, registered personally to Wing Commander Fielden, was little used and the first step towards disbanding the Flight was taken on February 14 1941 when it was sent to join the old Envoy at No 24 Squadron at the suggestion of the King. By now there had been a deliberate attack on Benson when a few incendiary bombs and 19 high explosives were dropped at just before 2 pm on January 30 and the three royal machines were kept at one side of the end hangar where Wellingtons and Spitfires from the Heston PRU were beginning to replace the former Fairy Battles.

The date of the departure for *King George VI,* a name proposed but never taken up for the Flamingo although on other work it was later to become *Lady of Glamis,* was significant because on the same day the Flight became the nucleus of No 161 Squadron augmented by personnel from No 138. The commander was Edward Fielden.

By now the former Flight was being dispersed. Corporal L. Trundle, the radio operator, and Aircraftsman G.P. Davis, engineer, had gone already, the remainder stayed until June when the two aircraft went, the Hudson to No 161 on the 22nd and so too air gunners Figg and Reid. In addition to these Flight Sergeants, Flight Engineer Jenkins also departed with a commission leaving Mr G.O. Peskett, Air Service Assistant Clerk, to be the last to leave on June 29.

The squadron of which the Captain of the King's Flight (the title was retained) took command at first operated from Gravely during March but after only about a month there a move was made to Tempsford, the bleak airfield which was to be its wartime home. Here with five Whitleys for parachuting agents into enemy territory and a single Wellington plus the Hudson, their work was (like that of No 138) the flying in of agents and supplies to occupied Europe. The agile Lysander was the type reserved for the most dangerous of these operations which called for actual landings under cover of darkness.

This type of sortie did not entirely take up the unit's time and the Whitleys were used to drop both leaflets and bombs. That carried out on the night of June 2 1942 saw the commander over enemy territory with his men during the bombing of Tours' marshalling yards. This was the first of a number of operations that found Wing Commander Fielden participating; and with the rank of Group Captain he found himself promoted to Station Commander on October 1, with Wing Commander Pickard, well known to the cinema-going public of those days from his role in *Target for Tonight*.

As the war situation changed there was still a need for the King to have a swift means of travel and therefore in his Court capacity of Flight Captain, Fielden was called to advise on a long flight which the Monarch was about to make. The aircraft type in which this was envisaged was a development of the Lancaster bomber with the same wings, powerplants and tail unit but a new and capacious fuselage. It was called the Avro York.

The third prototype, LV633, had been sent to No 24 Squadron at Hendon to serve as personal transport for the Prime Minister, Winston Churchill, who had made his first use of it to fly to North Africa on May 26 1943, the same day that it had been named *Ascalon*. On the return of this machine to Northolt, the captain was informed that it would be required before the week was out for the carriage of 'General Lyon'. That this was no more than a code name became obvious when Flight Lieutenant Jenkins was sent to examine the York in detail and the true identity of the passenger was confirmed at a flight briefing of the crew on June 11 by the AOC-in-C of Transport Command, then newly created, Sir Frederick Bowhill.

The arrival of George VI took place promptly at 8.30 pm, take-off was made half an hour later and course was set for North Africa via Gibraltar well out over the Atlantic where there would be less chance of encountering long-range Nazi aircraft. Strict radio silence was ordered but warships were stationed at the turning points and orders were issued that neutral Portugal was to be headed for in the event of engine failure.

Air Traffic Control at Gibraltar had wanted to divert the transport, along with many other Allied machines, ignorant of its importance, but by now *Ascalon* was in the circuit and ignoring orders to go elsewhere landed. It caused the CO some considerable surprise to find his King at his breakfast table, a fact that he at first refused to believe, thinking the announcement to be a joke dreamed up by his batman!

Less than an hour later, the big transport was on its way once more and finally landed at Maison Blanche in Algiers at 12.35 pm. Following a tour of the British First Army, despite an upset stomach

A visit to the Yeovil factory of the Westland Aircraft Company. The King is wearing Army uniform since the works was producing army co-operation machines at the time. He is escorted by Mr Eric Mensforth and Air Marshal Sir Wilfred Freeman (Imperial War Museum).

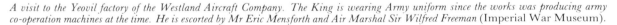

brought on by the long journey and the heat, King George next flew to Oran on June 14 to visit part of the US Fifth Army, and three days later a flight was made to Tunis. On June 19 the King was flown to Tripoli. Here, the crew of the Avro York were given seats in a car which was part of the motorcade through the city where the streets were lined by the victorious Eighth Army.

The flight home was begun from Tripoli on June 22 and was resumed two days later from Algiers. The trip went without a hitch but it was realised, well out over the Atlantic, that the time of arrival was set too far ahead. Consequently, mindful of meeting an escort of British fighters (USAAF P-38 Lightnings and P-39 Airacobras had performed this duty in Africa) not to mention welcoming parties, the engines were throttled back to kill time. The change in the note at once caught Fielden's ears and he hastened forward to enquire the reason. This was explained to him whereupon he ordered the captain to make all possible speed and not delay. The result was that the royal machine landed over an hour ahead of schedule, luckily to find the welcoming officers already in place, and it was only then that the line of Fielden's reasoning became apparent. He had conjectured that at no other point on the long journey were they so close to enemy airfields and he was determined to make maximum use of the brief hours of darkness that the summer night provided.

The following year a second flight on the same lines as the first was planned using the same machine, but this time the destination was to be Italy. After preliminaries similar to those which had gone before, the King arrived at Northolt on the evening of July 22 1944 with the Queen and Princess Elizabeth to see him off. The Royal party was about to board the York when the public air raid warning sounded and a V-1 flying bomb was heard approaching. Soon, the strange rattle of the flying bomb filled the air from a south-easterly direction and it was realised that it was far too late to conduct the royal group to cover which was some distance away. Nothing could be done and so the party merely stood by the aircraft and watched the spectacle of the small missile as it chugged overhead, lighting up the ground with the eerie light of its jet flame as it passed harmlessly out of sight.

When the machine finally took off at 11.10 pm the King was able to get some eight hours sleep and the crew flew with care knowing how important it was to His Majesty. These were the same men who had performed the previous mission, consisting of Wing Commander H.B. Collins, DFC, as captain with Wing Commander C.E. Slee, AFC, as additional pilot and Squadron Leader J.L. Mitchell, DFC, as navigator. A second pilot was carried in the form of Flight Lieutenant E.G. Fraser while the radio operators were Flight Lieutenant W. Gallagher and Flight Lieutenant S.S. Payne, DFM. The catering staff was, however, quite different and this was now in the hands of Flight Sergeant J. Duncan and Leading Aircraftsman W.T. Keates, the former later becoming very well known as Pan-America's commissariat manager at London Airport.

Following much the same route as on the previous trip *Ascalon* made landfall, after an eight-hour journey, at Rabat and, after breakfast, the flight was resumed to Naples. Here, King George changed aircraft and proceeded to his destination in *Freedom*, General Maitland Wilson's Dakota transport.

After an extensive tour of the Adriatic sector, taking in advanced units of the 8th Army as well as the RAF in addition to the Anzio beach-head and meeting various elements of the United States and Polish Armies, the King finally left for home on August 2. Although the actual take-off was delayed because the royal driver lost his way in the labyrinth of back streets behind the main thoroughfares of Naples, yet *Ascalon* arrived at Northolt exactly on time at 7.15 am on the morning of August 3—just as another flying bomb passed over. This was not the only use of an aircraft of the Avro York type by a member of the Royal Family during the war years, for Admiral of the Fleet, Lord Louis Mountbatten, used one numbered MW102 throughout the Burma campaign and indeed retained it after the war years when it was appropriately named *Viceroy of India*.

Trips by aeroplanes such as these which were made by the King were not the only examples of their wartime use by the Royal Family, and there were others interspersed with many visits to factories. This type of duty was one wherein the more advanced in age could compete with those in their prime and was an ideal means by which Her Majesty Queen Mary, widow of George V and therefore the Queen Mother, could give her support to flying although, like her husband, she never elected to fly. A typical example of this type of work was the visit, at the beginning of 1942, to the repair works at Rotol where she was able to inspect the work to reclaim airscrews. Occasionally Her Majesty showed that she was still spiritually youthful, however, as witness the occasion when, in an attempt to relieve an uneventful period of semi-evacuation in the following month, she requested that the detonation of a mine that had been washed ashore be delayed until she could be present. As a precaution, in case the weapon should be a 'dud', the officer and his men in charge of the disposal packed some extra explosive around the mine during the time gained. The resultant roar when the very live weapon was finally detonated was most satisfactory and before getting back into her car, Queen Mary thanked the bomb disposal party, not knowing the bit of 'stage management' they had provided!

Perhaps foremost among the other members of the Royal Family actively using the aeroplane as a means of expediting their war duties was the Duke of Kent, who, like his brothers, found the list of stations, factories and squadrons requiring his visits unending, not only in the British Isles but also abroad. An example was a trip in an American Liberator with his equerry, Wing Commander Sir Louis Greig, to inspect the Air Training Schools in Canada in the late summer of 1941, thus making the first royal flight across the Atlantic.

Sadly, aviation occasionally bites the hands which guide it, and thus it was with Prince George, a Wing Commander on the staff of the Inspection-General of the RAF. On August 25 1942 and, with a crew of ten, he boarded a Short Sunderland flying boat to travel to Iceland. It was a little before noon when the big machine with a full load of fuel and depth charges climbed away from Cromarty Firth and the pilot set course at an altitude of 1,500 feet. Shortly afterwards the first person to know that anything was wrong was a farmer who heard the machine roar overhead at a very low height, the noise of the engines being suddenly cut short by a massive crash followed by silence. He rushed to investigate, thinking to discover some vast hulk on the moors. In fact there was very little, the flying boat being broken into small parts scattered over a large area. There had been no explosion, the depth charges were intact and on the periphery of the chaos lay 11 bodies, among them that of the Duke of Kent, found lying in the heather so that he seemed to be asleep. The dead included the Unit Commander flying with the Duke and the only member of the crew to survive was the tail gunner later discovered, dazed, walking in the rain. A cross now marks the spot where Wing Commander, the Duke of Kent, and several other airmen died on duty that day.

'In the midst of life we are in death' and the responsibilities of the Royal Family had to go on with the necessary round of visits to RAF stations, aircraft works, airborne troops and also Bomber Command Headquarters while, in addition, civil authorities and the other three Services (including the Royal Marines) were not forgotten.

As the climax of the war in Europe approached, there were also changes in the manner of making royal flights taking place at home, although the final details of these were still the duty of Edward Fielden, in addition to his other work. He had been awarded the DFC in April 1943 and had become a Companion of the Victorian Order a little later. On the organisational side Hendon was the base from April 1944 for the newly-formed Metropolitan Communications Squadron with a wide range of equipment including DH89s, Hudsons, Oxfords, Ansons, Dakotas and 30 Percival Proctors among other machines; while the three Yorks that had performed such yeoman service were attached but

Prince George the Duke of Kent who was killed on active service on August 25 1942 when the Short Sunderland in which he was flying crashed in Scotland (Crown Copyright).

operated from Northolt. Among this collection of machines the former King's Flight Flamingo was retained for a time by No 24 Squadron and it was employed to take Queen Wilhelmina of the Netherlands on June 12 1944 from Hendon to Aldermaston. The type of work carried on is typified by the flight in Dakota FL559 that took Prince Bernhardt to the continent on March 19 1945, a trip with Flight Lieutenant J. Hubacek at the controls although, as a qualified pilot, the Prince made other journeys flying himself such machines as the Beechcraft Traveller (marked PB1) or PB2, his Lockheed 12A.

Changes continued to take place at an increased tempo as the Allied armies made their victorious progress on the Continent and it became evident that the war in Europe was nearly over. Not that this would bring any lessening of the calls on the Royal Family, these would probably be increased, and obviously the aeroplane was the only means whereby the coming programme of travels could be met. Early in 1945 the newly-promoted Air Commodore Fielden had been appointed to command the RAF base at Woodhall Spa but, by the summer, he had been moved again, this time to Transport Command Headquarters as Deputy Senior Air Staff Officer where his advice would be invaluable on matters connected with the King's travels, although the move was made for operational reasons, the Court duties only being a very minor part of Fielden's work.

The next problem which presented itself was the selection of a suitable machine for the work of royal visits for, although like his daughter, our present Queen, the King merely regarded air travel, not as an especial pleasure but rather as a swift means of completing a journey between two points, he would have been among the first to agree that no alternative existed that presented so many advantages.

Although there was no reason why His Majesty could not have borrowed the Prime Minister's *Ascalon,* once more the choice of a Dakota came as something of a surprise when orders were given for KN386 to be fitted out at No 5 Maintenance Unit at Kemble. The adantages of this selection were many, including the ready availability of spares. After the work was complete, the machine was delivered to No 24 Squadron at Hendon on the evening of June 6 1945, a swiftly-completed job as will be realised when it is stated that the aircraft had only been received from the US on March 4 after having been ferried across the Atlantic Ocean.

The morning following its delivery to No 24 Squadron, the Dakota, commanded by Squadron Leader S.A. Hinks, AFC, with Wing Commander T.H. Archbell, DFC, and Flying Officer W.G.R. Pearce making up the crew, left with the royal party at 9.45 pm for the first of its official trips, this one to visit the recently-liberated Channel Islands, and landfall was made one and a half hours later in Jersey. Following the visit here the King and Queen embarked once more at 3 pm to make the 20-minute journey to Guernsey where a welcoming salute was fired by the Royal Artillery using captured Nazi field guns! The return flight to Northolt was made at 6.25 pm.

Typical of the King's wartime duties was this visit to an airfield believed to be in the Eastern Counties. In the background is a Spitfire 9, MH765 ZD-X of No 222 Squadron, and in front a Typhoon Ib of No 183 Squadron, MN454 (Crown Copyright).

Opposite page top Ascalon, *the Avro York used for the historic wartime royal flights* (Imperial War Museum). **Centre** *Probably the first royal machine to have a highly-polished finish was Dakota KG770 used by King George and Queen Elizabeth to visit the Channel Islands* (Imperial War Museum). **Bottom** *Avro York* Endeavour, *the Duke of Gloucester's MW140* (Imperial War Museum).

Above *A change of uniform, but in RAF company, George VI with Winston Churchill and Trafford Leigh Mallory at AEAF Headquarters in 1944* (Imperial War Museum). **Below** *The Duke of Windsor visits an aircraft works on October 7 1945 and talks to the workers. Behind is a Dakota, KG624* (Crown Copyright).

After a short stay in the United Kingdom, the Duke of Windsor is seen off at Hendon by Air Commodore Fielden, Captain of the King's Flight. The date is October 11 1945 (Crown Copyright).

Another use of KN386 took place on June 13 when King George visited the RAF College at Cranwell in connection with its Silver Jubilee celebrations, the pilot on this occasion being Squadron Leader J.H.V. Millington, DFC. The royal party included Wing Commander Peter Townsend, DSO, DFC, an Extra Air Equerry, the distinguished Battle of Britain pilot, and Air Commodore Fielden.

Intensive use of aircraft such as this was not confined to the King alone among the royal brothers for, in his capacity as Governor-General of Australia, the Duke of Gloucester already had at his disposal an Avro Anson, an Avro York, MW140 *Endeavour,* and a Percival Proctor IV. Similarly, overseas royalty was making use of No 24 Squadron and on June 15, members of the royal family of Denmark were taken to Copenhagen by Flight Lieutenant G.H. Duncan in Dakota KJ981, while the similar FZ631 was used to take the Queen of the Belgians; a Belgian officer serving in the RAF, Squadron Leader J.A.M. Carlier, acting as captain.

July found KN386 in use once more, this time to take King George VI and Queen Elizabeth home again after a visit to the Isle of Man. Their Majesties made a similar flight, this time accompanied by Lieutenant, the Princess Elizabeth, when the landing was made at the aerodrome at Long Kesh in the hands of Squadron Leader S.R. Hinks who was also in charge for the return when a stop was made at Eglington.

The summer of victory year represented the high peak of the use of royal aircraft and thereafter employment of aeroplanes diminished. It became increasingly the custom to use the King's Dakota for VIPs, a practice which continued the manner of the use of earlier royal machines and which is still followed to this day.

However, there were other signs that aviation was to enjoy its royal patronage still and an example of this was when the Duke of Windsor, the former King Edward VIII, paid a visit to the British Isles in the later autumn of 1945. At the end of his stay, on October 11, he returned to France from the old, familiar RAF Station at Hendon and among those gathered to see him off was his former Flight Captain, Air Commodore E.H. Fielden, CVO, DFC, AFC, who had recently been awarded the Croix de Guerre by the Military Governor of Paris, General Joseph Pierre Koenig, in recognition of his wartime work in connection with the French Resistance Movement. Then, as 1945 moved towards its close, an important decision was taken; this was that the King's Flight, disbanded for most of the war years as an official unit, should be re-formed.

New Beginnings

'New beginnings spring from the end'
Pliny the Elder

By the beginning of the new year, 1946, it had been suggested that representations be made to His Majesty concerning the reformation of the Flight. King George approved this the following year, and at the same time confirmed the reappointment of Air Commodore E.H. Fielden, who had left the RAF during 1946, and had been awarded the CB, as the unit's captain. The question of suitable equipment had also come under tentative consideration.

The type of aircraft finally selected was a design which had been submitted by the Vickers company as early as 1944, conceived as an interim transport based on the wartime Wellington bomber, and the prototype had made its maiden flight at Wisley on June 22 the following year. Type designation was the VC1 but it was not long before it was named Viking.

In fact, the appearance of this machine, which still retained the geodetic construction wings of the bomber, now married to a fuselage covered in stressed skin, was surprisingly fortuitous since a production order for 50 was not long in being placed by the Ministry of Aircraft Production on April 5 and 19 days later the type's Certificate of Airworthiness was granted. On the following May 1 the reformed King's Flight came officially into being, its base to be its old wartime home of Benson which was by now a station of Coastal Command.

At this time plans were afoot for a royal visit to South Africa during the following year and this at once presented problems, for the original idea was that the aircraft should be of a special type designated the VVIP version. These would be operated in company with an Avro York similar to the design that had given such good service during the war years for trips to North Africa and Italy.

It immediately became obvious that the supply of the hoped-for machines was out of the question since although the establishment was at first for two special machines and one of the normal passenger version, this was later changed to include the addition of a freighter and workshop machine in August and it was quite impossible for anything like the work that was called for to be ready in time. The decision was therefore made that standard Vickers VC1s be delivered straight from the factory, a measure that would enable the flight crews to familiarise themselves with the type without delay.

The dispersal of the former King's Flight meant that not only had new aircraft to be selected but also personnel. This too came within the scope of Air Commodore Fielden's duties and for his deputy he chose a New Zealand officer, from Hastings. He was Wing Commander E.W. Tacon, MVO, DSO, DFC, AFC, who would act as Flight Commander. This very experienced officer had almost completed three tours of duty on wartime operations before being taken prisoner.

With all energies directed towards the forthcoming visit to the Union of South Africa, one of the first responsibilities of the new Flight Commander was to look into the airfields that might be used the next year and, with some of the new flight crew, he took a Viking to do this. Meanwhile the first machines to be taken on charge by the Flight began to arrive. VL245, the staff machine, since it required the minimum alteration from standard, appeared at RAF Benson on August 12 while the remaining three were delivered in the early part of the next year; VL246 for the use of the King, VL247 for Her Majesty and the workshop aircraft, VL248.

King George and Queen Elizabeth, together with their daughters, the Princesses Elizabeth and Margaret, embarked at Portsmouth for South Africa on February 1 1947 since the aircraft were to be used for internal journeys within the Union and not for the actual passage out, and the Vikings had therefore gone ahead earlier. The vessel used for the journey was HMS *Vanguard,* the newest of the Royal

Navy's battleships which had been named by the King's eldest daughter three years before.

The slower progress of the royal party obviated a problem that was to beset the aircraft crews soon after they had settled in at Brooklyn Air Station, which was to be their base near Cape Town for the duration of the tour. This was the sudden outbreak of sickness among both the air and ground crews, 20 in number, so that, averaging only four men to each machine, there were recurrent problems finding the manpower to keep the Vikings serviceable and clean. There is no doubt that this was entirely due to the speedy change of climate that the personnel had suffered.

In so vast a country, aircraft supplied the only means of covering anything like a representative cross-section for not only were there statesmen and officials to meet but also a certain amount of sight-seeing to be enjoyed. It was on a slippery climb up the Matopo hills that Princess Elizabeth passed her mother her own shoes and completed the ascent herself, unshod, commenting that it was much better that way as she had previously been taking four steps forward and sliding ten back! In all the Flight covered a distance of 160,000 air miles on the tour entirely without incident. The value of flights of this kind was not lost on the world's airline operators, for it is no coincidence that orders for the Viking took a sharp increase not long after and these included a demand for eight of the type from South African Airways.

The royal tour of the Union was completed during April and the journey home was made in *Vanguard* once again, but this in no way meant a

Above *Avro York C1, MW102, attached to No 48 Squadron at Seletar. It was used throughout and after the Burma campaign by Admiral of the Fleet Lord Louis Mountbatten* (L. Sorrell).

Left *Air Commodore Fielden (left), Captain of the King's Flight, and Wing Commander Tacon, the Flight Commander* (Photo News Ltd).

reduction in the royal use of the facilities of the Flight and these continued at home, in addition to the transportation of senior government officials, as had always been the case from the earliest days of even the private ownership by Prince Edward.

Interest in the King's Flight was not only stimulated abroad but at home also and the result of a Press visit to Benson was repeated in a wide variety of publications at the time. The number one saloon aft of the King's and of the Queen's machines was arranged to seat only four and behind this on either side were the toilets and steward's compartment. Number two saloon, like the royal one, was equipped with only four seats with wardrobes forming the divider between the fore and aft cabins. Immediately behind the flight deck was the commodore's quarters.

The internal arrangement of the staff aircraft was very similar to that found on a normal commercial Viking with similar seating but set out for only 20 persons so that wider spacing was possible between the pairs. Receiving the least comment, but perhaps the most vital machine of the whole group, was the workshop aircraft, the most noticeable feature of which was the work bench that ran down the starboard side at the rear of the rather spartan cabin. Along the wall above this work surface ran several lamps and points for power tools, ordinary hand tools being stored in a series of canvas bags with elastic tops ranged on transverse frames across the front fuselage.

As with any other 'airline' the King's Flight did not enjoy an exclusive period of trouble-free operation and an accident took place not long after the royal return from Africa. The machine involved was VL245—the staff aircraft—and it was this which was used while the Royal Family was in residence at Balmoral to deliver the mail from London. The Viking had reached Aberdeen and discharged its official freight, and had taken off once more from Dyce when it became necessary to make a forced landing. For this, the pilot picked out a suitable field and, despite the malfunctioning of a motor, the cause of the enforced descent, a good touchdown was made only to be spoilt when the aircraft struck a stone wall so that severe damage was sustained. The carrying out of repairs took some time and so, as a temporary measure, a standard machine of the same type was taken on charge by the Flight.

As events would have it, this service to deliver the official mail which never escapes members of the Royal Family, no matter where their place of residence, did give rise to an historic event in the further development of the services of the Flight because it was in order to expedite the transfer of letters from Dyce to Balmoral, where a cricket pitch was reserved as a suitable landing site, that Westland-Sikorsky R-4B 'Hoverfly' helicopters were added to the Vikings.

In fact there were three Hoverflys, all on loan from the RN, the first being KL110 which arrived on August 6 1947. This was followed two days later by KL106 whose stay, however, was to be brief for, ten days later, it suffered engine failure and had to be abandoned at Aberdeen. On August 25 this was replaced by another machine of the same type in the shape of KK973 and in company with the first Hoverfly this continued with the Balmoral mail delivery until September 30 when both aircraft were returned, KL110 to Brize Norton and KK973 to Feltham.

After the return from the royal tour of South Africa, considerable experience had been built up as to how best might aeroplanes be used for royal trips abroad, since it should be remembered that hitherto several machines of the same type, maintained and flown by a comprehensive staff of officers and men, had not been retained for work of this nature. So that, although they were able to draw on a fund of previous knowledge of various forms, Air Commodore Fielden and Wing Commander Tacon were still akin to pioneers in this field. In the immediate future, however, no great use of the aircraft was planned by the Royal Family but this is not to say that the Flight was idle: not only was there the work of flying cabinet ministers about to be done but there was also a set of special duties to be undertaken in November 1947. These were in connection with the marriage which took place in Westminster Abbey on the 20th of Princess Elizabeth to Lieutenant Philip Mountbatten, RN, who had relinquished his title of Prince and become instead the Duke of Edinburgh from that date. The work for the King's Flight on this happy occasion called for a considerable number of journeys to and from the Continent in order to collect and return the many royal guests who attended the wedding.

Afterwards little use was found for the Vikings but only because there was little flying at all in Great Britain that winter, which was the most severe in living memory. Even so, there was still plenty of administrative work to be done at Benson, for the bitter months were also those in which details were discussed and plans made for a new royal tour, based on that which had been carried out in South Africa, but covering a far greater area. This one was to take place at the end of 1948 and embrace New Zealand as well as Australia.

The previous tour had indicated that the ideal number of aircraft was five, not as had been used hitherto, and in consequence it was decided to

An historic machine—the Hoverfly helicopter—introduced for the delivery of mail to the Royal Family (Crown Copyright).

dispose of the machine that had been involved with the stone wall and replace it with two new ones, VL232 and VL233, both RAF Vikings.

Applying the lessons taught by the tour of Africa, November 29 was the day scheduled for the departure of the Viking fleet and the route covered staging points at Malta, Habbaniya, Karachi, Calcutta, Singapore and Darwin to Richmond, Australia, which was to act as the base. This return journey alone accounted for 26,000 miles.

The first machine away was to be the staff transport with baggage, police representatives and attendants, and the next Viking was to follow 20 minutes later. This was to be the first of the royal air liners and was to be followed, after a further delay of five minutes, by a second with Princess Margaret on board. After a 15-minute delay the machine carrying the staff alone would take off with the workshop Viking and spare aircraft bringing up the rear, so to speak, after a 25-minute interval.

The point to which the detail planning was taken is indicated by the fact that, at an average speed of 200 mph and an endurance of six and a half hours, it was estimated that a total distance of 4,345 miles had to be catered for over Australia and Tasmania, plus an additional 1,600 miles in New Zealand, the total flying time for the Royal Family being in the region of 30 hours. Naturally none of this could have been decided without practical inspection of the route and airfields and the late spring of 1948 had seen Air Commodore Fielden and Wing Commander Tacon making a detailed survey of the route and an associated proposed schedule by means of an actual proving flight, such as had been made to South Africa.

The following summer had also seen a resumption of the helicopter mail experiment with the temporary adoption once more of three Hoverflys. The first of these to join the Flight was KL110 again, on July 5, to be followed by July 10 by KK987 and on July 29 by KL104. As before all these had been made available on loan from the Royal Navy and, although KK987 was returned the following month, the others continued to deliver the mail to Balmoral until they, too, were sent back in October. All these Westland-Sikorsky machines came from the same small production batch totalling only 45 airframes. The historic and most-used KL110 was later to end its career in Canada.

However, on the human level there were other and graver events to mark 1948, for the closing months had seen an obvious deterioration in the health of King George VI although he still went about his public duties, and it was at about this time the author remembers the spontaneous gasp from a cinema audience at a close-up of the King's appearance in a news reel. In fact matters were as grave as they looked and even as the 28 officers and men of the Flight maintenance staff prepared to leave as the advance party, the King reluctantly took the advice of his doctors and it was announced that the proposed royal tour of Australia and New Zealand was postponed 'indefinitely'. In fact there was never to be another Commonwealth visit by His Majesty as his health was never again sufficiently robust to permit it.

In consequence of this sad state of affairs invitations to visit member countries of the Commonwealth tended to be made increasingly to Her Royal Highness Princess Elizabeth with her husband and, before long, tours were planned of Canada, with the disappointed Australia and New Zealand to follow. By this time, the Princess was an experienced air traveller as was right and proper for a Permanent Grand Master of the Guild of Air Pilots and Navigators, and in this capacity she had performed a naming ceremony nearly two years before when, at London Airport, a BOAC Avro Tudor had, with the aid of a bottle of Commonwealth champagne poured over its nose, become *Elizabeth of England.*

Quite naturally, flights to the more distant Commonwealth lands were beyond the scope of the equipment of the King's Flight which was still busy, although on a reduced schedule as it was now little used by either the King or Queen. Even so, there were other members of the family to be provided for including Princess Elizabeth who was frequently flown to Malta in one of the royal Vikings about this time and transportation for senior members of the government went on with quiet unobtrusiveness.

Although flying was the only practical way of reaching Canada in the post-war world, the distance involved was beyond the scope of the royal Vikings and resort had to be made to a commercial air liner. This was to be a Boeing Model 377 Stratocruiser, the individual machine being *Canopus.* The captain on this historic flight, important because of the fact that never before had a royal couple crossed the Atlantic by air, was O.P. Jones, the famous pilot who had been one of the central figures of the old Croydon-based days of Imperial Airways. The date was October 8 1951, the year of the Festival of Britain, when the giant air liner took off at 3 pm and set course out over the Atlantic with its escort of Avro Shackleton marine reconnaissance aircraft. These new machines, at the time representing the last word in coastal patrol efficiency, were not to be replaced until 1,300 miles had been covered when their place was taken by machines of the Royal Canadian Air Force. The final destination of *Canopus* was Montreal thus marking the start of a tour which was to include not only Canada but also a visit to Washington.

Of the round of events, meetings and presentations which marked the tour, a surprisingly large number had an aeronautical flavour. This trend seemed to be set at the very beginning when, on October 12, Princess Elizabeth and the Duke of Edinburgh attended a parade of the RCAF at Trenton, Ontario, where more than 700 officers and men were present. These were drawn up in the form of a gigantic 'V' along which the royal party passed during the inspection. The King's Colour and the Colour of the RCAF were carried in the parade by Flying Officers S. Woolley and D.C. McLeish respectively, the former standard being the same one that had been presented at a ceremony and drum-head service on Parliament Hill, Ottawa, during June 1950.

The highlight of the following tour included a visit to the Canadair Works where the production of North American F-86 Sabres took place, both for the Royal Air Force and the Royal Canadian Air Force. In order to cover the vast distances which the tour demanded, air transportation was once more called into use, the Canadian C-5, the modified model of the Douglas DC-5 Skymaster, being used.

Between the two royal tours which we have described there took place a great amount of that type of activity which had now become part of the routine of interest in aviation since the days of Edward VII. The journeys abroad were in fact merely the occasional highlight of this wider pattern. That the encouragement of an interest in all branches of aeronautics was not confined to only a few members of the Royal Family is shown by the presentation of a superb silver award, to be known as the Queen's Cup, to the flying model side of aeronautics by Her Majesty Queen Elizabeth, now the Queen Mother. She awarded the trophy personally on the first occasion in June 1948 and her son-in-law, the Duke of Edinburgh, became the first member of the family to use the King's Flight to take up a Service appointment when he flew to Malta to join his ship, the destroyer HMS *Chequers,* in October 1949. The next month found Queen Elizabeth inspecting an Auxiliary unit (which was now enjoying the title 'Royal' after the distinguished war performance of that force) when she was with No 600 'City of London' Squadron commanded by Squadron Leader D.E. Proudlove at Biggin Hill, Kent. The occasion was to mark Her Majesty's acceptance of the appointment as Honorary Air Commodore in the previous July.

Meanwhile the annual award of the Cup that had originally been presented by King George V was still competed for and the race that was to be flown from Wolverhampton Airport on June 17 1950 was of especial interest. This was due to the entry of a machine by Her Royal Highness Princess Margaret. Not that this alone was of great moment since Her Highness had entered for the previous year's contest with a Miles Whitney Straight which had only just failed to qualify for the final, but the 1950 entry attracted a peak of interest since the machine was the former PZ865, Hawker Hurricane F Mk IIC G-AMAU, formerly *The Last of the Many.* The pilot was Group Captain Peter W. Townsend who had flown the royal entry in 1949. He secured second place in an exciting contest and went on to fly this machine in a number of National Air Races at this period.

The pattern of royal journeys to various parts of the Commonwealth continued and, in 1952, it was decided that one should be carried out to East Africa as part of a wider tour planned to culminate in Australasia. By this time it was obvious that the King was not sufficiently recovered from a serious operation for lung resection to undertake the rigours of such a trip and once again the duty fell to Princess Elizabeth and her husband.

As before, a commercial air liner was to be used to take the royal couple from London Airport, this time an Argonaut from the BOAC fleet named *Atalanta* and registered G-ALHK. This machine was drawn up on the tarmac on a chilly day, January 31 1952, a little before mid-day and it was not long before the royal party began to arrive, consisting of King George VI, Queen Elizabeth and Princess Margaret to see the Princess and Duke off on what was to be a five-month tour. Farewells were said, the door of the Douglas DC-4 closed and the steps drawn away. At the controls Captain R.C. Parker, who was to pilot the Argonaut as far as El Adem, opened the motors up and slowly the big four-engined machine began to roll forward. The King, his hair ruffled in the January wind, lifted his arm to wave—there were those who said afterwards that to do even this was an effort—and the liner gathered speed and lifted into the afternoon sky.

Aviation arrangements for this tour differed in some ways from those for the trips carried out earlier. There was certainly occasion to cater for some internal flying once Nairobi was reached and to perform these journeys a Dakota, RMA *Sagana,* was to be used, flown by the deputy manager of the owner company, A.N. Francombe, a former Wing Commander. Nothing that planning and experience could foresee had been left to chance, and with Captain R.G. Ballantyne taking over for the second leg of the outward journey, all seemed set fair for another successful royal tour in which the aeroplane would take an important part.

The royal couple had carried out only a few of the duties on the very full programme when grave news from London was telephoned to the Duke of Edinburgh in East Africa; King George VI had died suddenly in his sleep the night before and had been found by a horrified valet the next morning. The girl who had left London Airport a Princess was to return a Queen.

The sad journey home was completed on February 7 and the same air liner that had been flown on the departure was used. As it taxied in, the guard of honour found by the RAF was brought to attention and Clement Attlee and Winston Churchill waited at the foot of the aircraft stair as a small figure dressed in mourning appeared at the door of the *Atalanta*: but there was no pleasure in the minimum ceremonial for the atmosphere seemed to reflect the sadness that stopped even BBC broadcasts of all but news bulletins on that day. At the funeral of the first King to be a qualified Royal Air Force pilot, his adopted Service was represented in force and marched in slow time with firearms reversed as had their fathers in an earlier cortège.

Following the Coronation of the new Queen, on a rather wet June 2 1953, a series of announcements was issued from Buckingham Palace concerning future appointments which it usually follows are filled by the monarch. Of these, Her Majesty had agreed to accept the position of Air Commodore-in-Chief of the Royal Auxiliary Air Force, the Royal Air Force Regiment and of the Royal Observer Corps, while the similar appointment to the Air Training Corps, like the others formerly held by the late King, was now taken over by the Duke of Edinburgh. As may be imagined, all these appoint-

Below left *The BOAC Argonaut air liner in which Princess Elizabeth flew to Africa in 1952—and returned a Queen* (British Airways).

Right *The second Royal Review of the RAF, this time to mark the Coronation of HM Queen Elizabeth II—an aerial view of the assembly* (Crown Copyright).

ments imposed a new demand on the services of the re-named Queen's Flight. The commander was now Wing Commander J.E. Grindon, DSO, AFC, serving under Air Commodore Fielden who was confirmed in his post as Captain of the Flight and had been created GCVO in the previous year, and he continued to supervise the many journeys made with the aid of the Flight, in connection with the new appointments in particular and the accession in general.

Meanwhile Her Majesty's connections with the Royal Air Force continued to be strengthened and not all of these entailed the use of aeroplanes to travel to a distant station. One that fell into the category of 'London venue' was in many ways unique. This was the presentation of the Colour to the Royal Air Force Regiment to mark the tenth anniversary of the formation of the unit. Indeed, the formulation of the Queen's Colour and the approval of the design by Her Majesty were among the earliest duties of the Queen.

The actual presentation ceremony was probably historically significant since when it took place, on March 17 1953, it was conducted in the Ballroom at Buckingham Palace and it is believed, as far as records show, that never before had Colours been presented in that room.

Since the Regiment is a mobile unit its Colours are unusual in that they are not confined to the British Isles as are those of the Royal Air Force in the United Kingdom, Cranwell and Halton. These had been presented by Princess Elizabeth due to her father's ill health on July 6 1948, May 26 1951 and July 25 1952. It is not, therefore, surprising that the Queen's Colour of the Regiment should feature in the ceremonial that marked the following year in several parts of the world. These included the unveiling of the El Alamein Memorial on October 24 1954 and in the previous July when Princess Margaret paid a visit to RAF and Army units in Germany. But the first appearance of the new Colour was during May of that year when it was paraded after an air journey to the Middle East to mark the arrival in El Adem of the Queen and the Duke of Edinburgh.

By now, His Royal Highness had the right to wear pilot's wings when he appeared in uniform, since the previous months had seen him engaged in an intensive programme of training. This had begun on November 12 1952 with a flight in a standard de Havilland DHC1 Chipmunk, WP861, under instruction from 29-year-old Flight Lieutenant Caryl Ramsay Gordon, a native of Cheltenham. WP912 was also used on some later occasions, and on December 20 the Duke went solo on this type, from Bircham Newton, near Sandringham.

Although this milestone had been passed there was still more instruction to be taken and the second week in February found the Duke, now a Marshal of the RAF, like his late father-in-law and the Duke of Windsor, working on stalls and forced landings, taking over a North American Harvard, KF725, later the same month. At the end of April it was announced that he would be graduating to twin-engined aircraft and this he did on an Airspeed Oxford from White Waltham aerodrome before finally being awarded his 'wings' at a private ceremony conducted at Buckingham Palace on the afternoon of May 4 1953. The actual presentation was made by Chief of the Air Staff, Air Vice-Marshal Sir William Dickson in the presence of the Queen, some senior RAF officers and Flight Lieutenant Gordon. The successful completion of the course was not achieved without its irritations since continuity had been difficult because of the interference by over-cautious officials and it was even necessary at one stage for the Duke to enlist the aid of Sir William Dickson to combat this.

By the time that the Queen was crowned, the Duke was therefore a qualified RAF pilot. There is on record a story that he had refused to pose for official photographs wearing a Service jacket adorned with 'wings' even though assurances were given that the prints would not be released until the course of instruction was successfully completed. With a fairly comprehensive knowledge of the problems involved by this time, the Duke was in a position to admire the airmanship of the fly past made to mark the day and which he witnessed with other members of the Royal Family from the balcony of Buckingham Palace as the formations swept low over the Mall.

It was about this time that a curious tale was in circulation to the effect that the Duke of Edinburgh was to be dissuaded from flying either as pilot or passenger in a jet aircraft. One imagines that it would be an achievement to persuade Prince Philip to take any course of action against his better judgement but, apart from that, the story was not even true; what had in fact been said was that it would be 'inappropriate'—at that point in time—to offer the Duke a flight in a jet, a very different thing, as the technical press of the period pointed out.

The very full schedule of the royal year, 1953, continued to make its demands on different members of the Royal Family and the same month that had seen the Coronation found Queen Elizabeth, the Queen Mother and Princess Margaret on a trip to Southern Rhodesia. Naturally a journey of this nature was beyond the range of the machines of the Queen's Flight and therefore the flight was made in a commercial air liner, a de Havilland Comet, the first jet propelled aircraft to enter regular scheduled service anywhere in the world.

The chosen machine was G-ALYW commanded by Captain A.P.W. Cane and, with other members of the Royal Family at London Airport to bid mother and daughter farewell, the machine began the 6,071 mile journey at 1.15 pm on Tuesday, June 30. Flying at an average altitude of 34,000 feet, the first stop was at Rome and it left there after an hour's break to land at Beirut, 6 hours and 40 minutes after leaving London. Arriving at Khartoum early the following morning, a new crew under Captain E.E. Rodley took over to fly the jet to the penultimate stop at Entebbe where the royal party had breakfast at Government House.

The final landing at Salisbury took place at 9.52 am on Wednesday, July 2, and eight minutes later the steps were in position, the doors were opened, and the Queen Mother and Princess Margaret were ready to disembark. On Friday, July 17 the royal pair were home again in the same machine having left Salisbury at 8.15 the previous day, 'It has been a wonderful trip', said the Queen Mother later, 'I have great personal faith in the Comet'.

As 1953 drew towards its close it was reckoned that the time was near when certain machines of the Queen's Flight were coming to the end of their effective term of service and steps were taken to dispose of them. The first of these was the subject of a confidential investigation into its possible value taken early in September, the aircraft in question being VL248, the workshop machine that had been one of the original Vikings sent to South Africa. At the time the airframe was in course of being modified to standard configuration after a total of 802 hours 15 minutes flying time, 3 hours 45 minutes of which had been since the last major inspection by Vickers Limited, while the motors then fitted had both flown 55 minutes since overhaul by Bristol. These totals may appear small and by comparison with the flying time accumulated by commercial machines of the same sort, which were averaging some ten times this number of hours, they certainly were but the type had joined the Flight on January 21 1947 and since it was poor publicity for a Head of State to be visiting countries abroad in a design six years old, a gradual replacement with more up to date types was envisaged. Thus it was that this, the first of the Vikings to go, was eventually sold to Mexican Air Lines.

There were other changes in the air as 1953 entered its final months, but as yet they were no more than officially unconfirmed reports. The most persistent of these was that the Duke of Edinburgh had requested that a landing ground be sought near to the centre of London in order that he might use this form of travel to keep official engagements in South East England.

At the end of Coronation year this, and items like it, was no more than a tale passed on verbally, for at the time there were other, and considerably greater,

Right *Queen Elizabeth with Prince Philip on the saluting base at RAF Odiham for the Coronation Review. On the extreme left stands Air Chief Marshal the Duke of Gloucester while on the right are Boeing Washingtons (B29s)* (Crown Copyright).

Right *Gloster Meteor NF11 fighters of No 29 Squadron during the Coronation Review flypast at Odiham. 'Never has such impeccable formation flying been seen before', wrote a witness* (Hawker Siddeley).

Below *VL248 in later insignia at the time of the proposed visit to Australia and New Zealand* (Photo News Ltd).

Queen Elizabeth with RAF officers at Odiham during the 1953 Coronation Review. In the background are Avro Anson trainers (Crown Copyright).

events taking place in the aviation world as patronised by the Royal Family. Chief among these was to be the historic royal tour of the world covering 20,000 miles by air, the first time that a reigning monarch had carried out such a tour.

The original request that air transport be used to cover such distances as the 10,000 miles called for by only the visit to Australia, had come personally from Her Majesty. It must be admitted that, although she is an enthusiast for the convenience offered by air travel, it is other members of her family who are keen on flying for its own sake. The tour began on the evening of November 23, inevitably at London Airport when the Queen with the Duke of Edinburgh left in the familiar G-AKGN *Canopus* once more.

It was on this marathon journey that the Queen had her first experience of a trip in a four-engined type that was to figure increasingly in the story of the Royal Flight which was still to come, the design being the de Havilland Heron. The particular occasion was to take place at Rotorua in New Zealand when Her Majesty used an aircraft of this type to fly to Gisborne, the actual aircraft being one of the fleet of New Zealand National Airways. The design in question was little more than a four-motor variant of the smaller, twin-engined Dove and one of these had been temporarily attached to the Queen's Flight since the previous summer when VP961 had been sent to Benson for the use of the Duke of Edinburgh, who was using the type to increase his hours on a multi-engined aircraft.

During 1954, which saw the Queen and her consort home after their demanding tour, the normal work of the Flight continued at something of an increased tempo, not only providing facilities for Her Majesty but also for government ministers and the remainder of the Royal Family. Perhaps typical of the latter was the trip undertaken in one of the Vikings by the Queen Mother, still soberly-clad since the death of her husband, when VL247 took her from London Airport to Wick, the type of journey which was to assist her to make history in the near future.

The next major use of the Flight by the Queen personally took place in the late summer of that year when she flew to Driffield, Yorkshire, to spend a short holiday with Sir Richard and Lady Sykes. As the two previous monarchs had been when making a journey by air, she was accompanied on the trip and during the inspection of the RAF guard of honour by Air Commodore Edward H. Fielden, KCVO, CB, DFC, AFC, who had now been awarded a knighthood for his long and outstanding service to the Crown. One of the innovations that he had recently seen was the introduction that year of a helicopter on to the strength of the Queen's Flight. Hitherto this type of aircraft had been used only for the transport of mail but, with the addition of a Westland Dragonfly HC4, a step had been taken towards the use of the type for taking passengers. This was XF261 and, although a new step was thus taken in the maintenance of progress at the Benson unit, it was not until the next year that the larger strides were to be made.

Meanwhile, 1954 was to mark a very important point in the piloting career of the Duke of Edinburgh, for early October was to find him at West Raynham RAF Station once more in the company of Flight Lieutenant Gordon. The purpose of this was to enable the Duke to become familiar with the operation of jet aircraft and it was from here that he flew a total of 1 hour 35 minutes on two occasions in a two-seat Gloster Meteor twin-motor jet trainer. In addition, the Duke also took advantage of his holiday at Balmoral to familiarise himself with the position of several northern air-fields, using RAF Edzell as a base for this work, the aircraft flown being his personal Heron machine.

Wingèd Sandals

'Let us look for our wingèd sandals'
Cicero

Two years after the coronation of Her Majesty the Queen a series of events were to take place that changed the entire nature of the Flight. The first signs of this change were to be seen as early as April of that year when the Queen Mother, as their Honorary Air Commodore, paid a visit to Biggin Hill in Kent where Nos 600 and 260 Squadrons of the Royal Auxiliary Air Force were stationed. What caused some comment in the Press of the time is that the journey from Windsor was made not by road but by helicopter, the first time that she had travelled in this way.

The machine used for this historic flight was an S-55 of the Fleet Air Arm. It had taken off from Smith's Lawn which had seen so much use for aeroplanes from the earliest days of flying. On arrival at Biggin Hill, Her Majesty was greeted by Air Vice-Marshal H.L. Patch, AOC of No 11 Group, before reviewing a parade and watching a fly-past which was followed by a demonstration of Bofors-gun drill by the RAF Regiment Squadron. After tea and a visit to the Chapel she was in the air once more and was deposited back at Windsor, all within three hours of her departure. Two days later the Queen again made use of a helicopter, this time a Dragonfly, to travel to Tidworth and by these two trips joined that small group of royal helicopter passengers which included Princess Margaret, who had flown in this manner on the Continent, and the Duke and Duchess of Gloucester. These were not alone for the Duke of Edinburgh had also travelled to official engagements in a helicopter so that there was little surprise in the announcement during June of that year that he had already begun a course of instruction in flying this type of aircraft, receiving training from Lieutenant-Commander M.H. Simpson, the Chief Flying Instructor of No 705 Squadron at Gosport. This was a logical development since it was in a Westland Whirlwind from this unit, piloted by Lieutenant-Commander John Jacob, that the Duke had been making most of his official visits for some time, although the instructional machine was a Dragonfly from which His Highness soon graduated to the larger type.

In the light of these events it is hardly surprising that little time would elapse before persistent rumours preceded official announcement that, in the near future, three rotary-wing machines would be joining the Queen's Flight and the only delay was in the selection of a suitable design. In fact some three years were to pass before this was to take place.

Meanwhile other innovations were about to be made and in the middle of May de Havilland Heron C3, XH375, was sent to Benson where it was designated the Duke of Edinburgh's personal machine. Only a few days before delivery, the Duke had gained some experience at the controls of the company's demonstrator machine, G-AMTS. He flew from White Waltham and back from Cornwall in the company of Flight Lieutenant Gordon, being airborne for more than three and a half hours. This widening of air experience only befitted a senior officer who had, only a few weeks before, consented to become Patron of the British Gliding Association and who, on December 16 of the same year, was to deliver at Church House, Westminster, the Tenth British Commonwealth and Empire Lecture to the Royal Aeronautical Society, taking as the subject of his paper 'Aviation and the Development of Remote Areas'. His personal experience was of use here and formed the outline to the beginning of his talk.

By now the Duke of Edinburgh was adding considerably to his flying hours and for this the de Havilland Heron, of which delivery had been taken personally from Sir Geoffrey de Havilland on May 18, had been in steady use. Its markings, as if to emphasise the fact, had undergone a change to Service type insignia and a serial number—XH375—appeared in place of the makers' designation G-5-7 which had previously been carried. It was this

Left *Sir Geoffrey de Havilland hands over Heron C3 XH375 to the Duke of Edinburgh on May 18 1955* (Hawker Siddeley).

Opposite page *de Havilland Heron XH375 in flight over Windsor Castle* (Hawker Siddeley).

machine, in company with the two Vikings VL246 and 233, which were the most frequently used aircraft of the Flight at this time.

Meanwhile there were small but important changes taking place within the Royal unit and in September Wing Commander D.F. Hyland-Smith, DFC, AFC, took over as Flight Commander and in the following month Group Captain J.E. Grindon, the previous commander and personal pilot to the Queen, departed to take up a new appointment as commander of RAF Honington. This vacancy had been created by the promotion to SHAPE of Group Captain Clayton who had previously been in charge of the RAF Station, and a new post was created in November when it became clear that the constant use which was now being made of the Flight would demand the services of a Deputy Captain.

The establishment of the Queen's Flight stood at a mere 80 officers and men at the time of Her Majesty's inspection of the unit which took place on November 2 following the command changes. The inspection was carried out by the Queen alone for her husband was half a world away, in fact in Australia to perform the opening of the Olympic Games in Melbourne on November 22. It was now quite naturally accepted that he would journey to this part of the Commonwealth by air and so the departure from London Airport on October 15 excited no more than the usual interest. The outward journey had been made in one of British Overseas Airways Corporation's DC-4 Argonaut air liners and *Ajax* finally set down in Mombasa where the Duke found the Royal Yacht waiting for him, in which he was to complete the trip.

Although a celebration of sport, the events surrounding these Olympic Games enjoyed a particularly aviation atmosphere. The Duke had flown in a highly-polished Handley Page Hastings of the Far East Transport Wing from Butterworth to Kuala Lumpur where it made use of the specially extended runways which had only recently been completed. Even the actual journey to the opening ceremony of these Games had been made by air when a Convair 440 of the Royal Australian Air Force had flown the Duke from Canberra to the stadium at Melbourne. The previous day had also seen him at the same aerodrome but this time boarding a Douglas DC-3 Dakota belonging to the Royal Australian Navy which, with an escort of Hawker Sea Furies, was to take the Duke on a visit to Nowra Naval Air Station lying 90 miles south-west of Sydney. This was to see the work of the school of aircraft maintenance together with that of the school of anti-submarine warfare operated jointly by the RAAF and the RAN. But it was by helicopter that the Duke of Edinburgh was to fly to inspect the naval and air installations at Jervis Bay before returning to Canberra. But the final royal aviation note for 1956 was to be struck not by the Duke but by Princess Margaret who, for part of her visit to British Africa at the end of the year, used the Flight's Heron aircraft.

Home once more from the Olympics, Prince Philip at once embarked on a refresher course in flying this type of machine and, with Squadron Leader B.G. Stanbridge in the co-pilot's seat, did some night flying from White Waltham using the Blackbushe night-landing aids early in March of the following year.

The reason for this delay in once more getting to the controls of the new type was in no way due to winter weather but because other pressing duties (a

problem throughout the Duke's flying training) prevented an earlier resumption. However, it was not only familiarisation with the flying of conventional aircraft which was undertaken that spring for, in the middle of that May, the Duke of Edinburgh had carried out his first flight in a glider. This had been undertaken at the headquarters of the Bristol Gliding Club at Nympsfield near to Stroud, Gloucestershire, in a Slingsby T42 belonging to Peter Scott, the artist and ornithologist, who founded the Slimbridge Severn Wild Fowl Trust where Prince Philip was staying at the time.

Accompanied by a club instructor, Peter Collier, the flight had been carried out in somewhat unfavourable conditions since it was very gusty and the trip lasted no more than eight minutes. Even so the pair were lucky to reach an altitude of 2,000 feet with the aid of a thermal discovered at the top of the launch at about 800 feet, and it was decided to return to Nympsfield because a cross-country flight might have prevented their return. Later that year the Duke flew a Slingsby T42 Eagle glider from Lasham when he was towed aloft by a Tiger Moth during the National Gliding Championships.

The next year found Prince Philip in a very different aviation setting when at RAF Wyton in Huntingdonshire. From this station he flew for the first time in a Vulcan bomber with Wing Commander Frank Dodd, the Officer Commanding No 230 Operational Conversion Unit, at the controls. During the flight Prince Philip, who was in the co-pilot's seat, took over the controls of the bomber several times. The primary object of the visit to the station had been a tour of inspection where the three 'V-bombers' of the day were to be seen, the Vickers Valiant, Handley Page Victor and Avro Vulcan. The inevitable display of a 'scramble' by the crews of five Valiants of No 543 Squadron had been included. The Duke's destination in the bomber flight that followed was Farnborough where a fast letdown was made from 40,000 feet at which altitude most of the journey had been carried out. The subsequent landing had been completely radar-controlled from the approach onwards and was the culmination of a simulated attack on an Andover. But perhaps of greater historical moment was the fact, which did not go unnoticed by the servicemen gathered there that day, that when all was over the Duke departed in a helicopter piloted by himself as had been the case on arrival. The bomber was XA900 and the date had been June 24.

Events such as this were typical of 1958 which was one of great importance in the royal aviation calendar. Perhaps the first of these had taken place as early as March when Queen Elizabeth the Queen Mother was at the end of a five-week tour of Australia and New Zealand and is an example of one of those chapters of minor accidents which beset us all. The trip had covered a total of 25,000 miles and it was now time for Qantas to bring the Queen Mother home. Sensible of the need to make sure that every forseeable contingency was catered for, Qantas seemed to have made sure the flight would proceed without a hitch, only for all the effort to go for nought in a set of unrelated happenings that reflected in no way on the efficiency of the organisation.

The first of these had taken place on March 7 in the shape of an engine failure by the No 3 Wright Turbo-Compound motor when the aircraft was over the Indian Ocean and heading for the Cocos Islands. At the time it was announced that this had been brought about by a break in the cylinder-head damaging the cowling. This was almost in the style of a modern version of 'for want of a nail' for the machine had to be diverted to Mauritius and, as a result, Her Majesty was prevented from performing the opening ceremony the following day of Nairobi's new airport at Embakasi.

It was the same motor which brought about the next delay when ignition trouble at Entebbe wasted 18 hours in diagnosis and elimination so that it was deemed wiser for a Bristol Britannia of BOAC to be flown out to pick up the Queen Mother. However, she had no intention of deserting her Australian crew and remained until the fault was finally cleared. Nevertheless, it almost seemed to be fated that Her Majesty was not to come home in the care of Qantas for hardly had all seemed well and the royal passenger re-embarked when the machine developed a hydraulic fault at Malta. It was here that the Queen Mother had reluctantly to decide in favour of the Britannia in the light of the fact that the series of events had now totalled a delay of four days. Thus ended the unhappy saga of events, probably unique in the history of the company.

March saw the long-anticipated change in equipment of the Queen's Flight that had been foreshadowed by the acquisition of the de Havilland Heron type, with the announcement that the three remaining Vikings were to be phased out. In fact they had not long to go for, in April, they were sold to Tradeair and their place was taken by a pair of Herons which received the designation C4, indicating their being to the latest production standards. These were XM295 and 296 and, externally, they presented few differences from Prince Philip's XH375 except that the new machines had a broad cheat line of Royal Blue down the polished dural and white fuselage side, whereas the Duke's machine was still distinguished by a similar band of Edinburgh Green.

A Stratocruiser similar to Canopus *much used on world flights by Queen Elizabeth* (British Airways).

The summer of 1958 brought with it the announcement that Air Chief Marshal, the Duke of Gloucester, was to be promoted to the rank of Marshal of the Royal Air Force with effect from June 12. He had held his former appointment since 1944 having previously been an Air Marshal for three years and held the rank of Air Vice-Marshal since 1937. Meanwhile Princess Margaret was still engaged in a series of visits to Commonwealth countries and, during her stay in Canada later the same summer, she had flown over the St Lawrence Sea-way in the co-pilot's seat of a Canadair C-5 of the Royal Canadian Air Force with Wing Commander W.K. Carr at the controls.

Herons were now proving their worth as the new type for the Queen's Flight and they were to take part in a number of major tours, one of them before the year which had seen their introduction had run its course. As coincidence would have it this event also involved the Duke of Gloucester who, with the Duchess, used the type to visit Ethiopia, British Somaliland and Aden towards the end of the year, going on to Nigeria in 1959. Yet despite all such events as these, the hindsight of history must see 1958 as the year of the helicopter for the Queen's Flight.

The first move was the replacement of the Dragonfly by a single Whirlwind, in fact an HAR4 completed to ordinary Service standards, in the identity of XL111, and this was still in use in September when it was officially announced that two similar machines were on order. In fact the specification for these had been drawn up a little earlier and they were to have basic Whirlwind HAS7 airframes but be given the designation Mk 8 to cover the special furnishings, dual controls and the alteration of the normal seating from eight to four. But such is the way of things that these historic machines were not to reach the Queen's Flight until more than a year later when Whirlwind HCC8s XN126 and 127, brought up to VVIP standards, were received in November 1959.

In all major respects these two differed not at all from the Series 2 type sold on the civil market or the Service version in use by the Fleet Air Arm and they were powered in exactly the same manner too by an Alvis Leonides Major engine which was now standard and derated to deliver 750 hp. Naturally what changes there were all contributed to adapting the internal arrangement for the work in hand or the safety measures and those inside were designed about the pair of Rumbold seats for the main passengers. In front of these was a similar pair for the use of equerries and these could be arranged to face either forward or to the rear. A further grouping allowed an extra two flight chairs in a unit towards the front of the cabin for attendants if required and these, like the seating for the equerries, had to be offset to the port side in order to permit sufficient space immediately inside the entrance door on the starboard side. Alternatively eight persons could be carried, three facing forward and five aft. A concession to the use of the helicopters by ladies was the provision of two fixed steps below the door sill and a handrail.

The two main flight controls' hydraulic booster systems already in use in the HAS7 and Series 2 models were combined as an emergency precaution on these HCC8s so that the twin pumps remained independent and were driven from the transmission.

Westland Whirlwind HCC8, XN126, in company with XN127 of similar vintage, both displaying a change of colour scheme (Crown Copyright).

Moreover, should the occasion demand, engine oil could be used to power the lateral controls with manual for the longitudinal and collective control. In an emergency it was also possible for the pilot to eject an automatic six-man dinghy which could be stowed in a ventral compartment. This arrangement made as sure as possible that the chance of damage to the dinghy was minimised in the event of the helicopter turning over in an emergency ditching.

It was also possible for a 70 lb winch capable of lifting 400 lb with the aid of its integral hydraulic motor to be bolted forward above the entrance door and two control points were provided, one on the top of the pilot's control column and the other at the end of a flexible lead permitting operation from the main saloon. All other changes were of a relatively minor nature and included some chromium-plated fittings, fresh air intakes and locking caps for the fuel fillers, while landing flares could be fired in an electric discharger aft of the cabin, offset below the starboard side, and flashing beacons were mounted above and below the fuselage.

However, despite the designation it would be quite wrong to assume that this, or any other aircraft of the Flight, was utilised for the transportation of royalty alone. The idea behind the specifications at their formulation was that a machine be available for any of a multitude of duties so that in one sense Her Majesty's aeroplanes can never be more than in the general purpose category. Here an illustration is provided by the fact that in these Westland helicopters the constant shifting of ballast as demanded by the helicopter's use is obviated by a quantity being permanently fitted in the tail-rotor boom and in the strut of the tail bumper.

All this was, however, still in the future when 1958 drew towards its close but the year had one more royal aviation connotation, an event which had been long awaited. This was the reconsecration of Wren's church of St Clement Danes in the Strand. When, on a night in the 'blitz' full of flame and horror, the famous bells of nursery legend had crashed down to their destruction at the foot of the tower, it seemed as if the church that dated from 1681 had gone for ever. But the next morning when the walls and steeple were seen to be standing men began to hope. There had been a place of worship on the site near Temple Bar since the ninth century when the number of Danes buried there had given its peculiar name; even the fabric demolished by Christopher Wren to make way for his own design had dated from the 14th centrury. Then, 17 years after the London 'blitz', that hope was justified when, on a chill October Sunday, the Bishop of London consecrated the edifice again and thus ensured that for all time the church would be that of the Royal Air Force. It was during the service in the presence of Her Majesty Queen Elizabeth II and His Royal Highness the Duke of Edinburgh that the 'sentence of consecration' was signed by the Bishop and passed to the Chaplain-in-Chief of the Royal Air Force. Since this was a legal document it ensured that the new role of the church in caring for the Books of Rememberance recording the names of the Service's 125,000 dead would continue in perpetuity. During the ceremony, the Queen was able to hear the re-cast bells peal out the March of the Royal Air Force and by her presence made the day more than just another royal aviation ritual, for it was a continuance of the many connections with flying that have been maintained from the days of 'Edward the Peacemaker'. But perhaps the nearest parallel was with the unveiling performed by her uncle after the earlier war when the flags had been slipped from the memorial, which had stood since 1923 a short way off, to reveal the great bronze eagle by Conrad Parlanti. Her father had also maintained the connections in a similar way when he had opened the Royal Air Force Chapel in Westminster Abbey on July 10 1947, the seventh anniversary of the first day of the Battle of Britain.

The presence of Her Majesty and Prince Philip at St Clements marked perhaps fittingly the concluding weeks of a year of royal connection with the RAF; a period which had begun with the Queen's attendance at Bentley Priory for the 40th anniversary dinner on April 1. This was her second visit to the home of Fighter Command and Headquarters of the former Inland Area, since she had previously been to the Priory as Princess Elizabeth in 1950. She thus established one of the patterns of her reign which was to follow, one of the earliest attendances at a Royal Air Force ceremonial after her accession being the unveiling of the Imperial War Graves Commission's Runnymede Memorial on May 13 1953.

Undoubtedly the premier aircraft of the 1950s was the de Havilland 106 Comet. This type had entered service with BOAC on May 2 1952 and thus became the first turbojet aircraft anywhere in the world to operate on regular scheduled commercial services. Although setbacks, inevitable in any pioneer scheme in any field of endeavour, had followed, the use of the type in such a bold manner had secured for it a permanent place in history. A second achievement was the modification of the Comet Series 2 for service with the RAF so that it also marked the first use of a pure jet aircraft for military transport. Transport Command took delivery of their first Comet as early as July 7 1956.

The early flight in a Comet by the Queen Mother and Princess Margaret has already been described but the first flight in one of these jets for Her Majesty the Queen and Prince Philip was to be carried out in one of the RAF machines on June 4 1957—less than a year after the introduction of the type into use by Transport Command. At the time the Royal Family was in residence at Sandringham so the obvious point of embarkation was RAF Marham in Norfolk. Take-off on this historic Tuesday was made at exactly 10.31 am and the journey to Leuchars, Fife, was completed in 55 minutes. The purpose of the flight was to present a Standard to No 43 Squadron and when the ceremony and inspection were over the Queen and the Duke left for London Airport, once more in the Comet C2 from No 216 Squadron, captained by Squadron Leader D.J. Harper, arriving at Heathrow 1 hour and 12 minutes after leaving Scotland.

By this time all but one of the ten RAF Comets had been delivered and it was in one, also of No 216 Squadron, that the Queen Mother and Princess Margaret flew to Rome a little later, the Captain in this case being Squadron Leader E.P. Pullan. In 1959 the Duke of Edinburgh flew to India and Pakistan in a Comet and later joined Queen Elizabeth for a crossing of the Atlantic in a BOAC machine of the type. By this time the Royal Family's use of jets had largely ceased to merit attention by the news media although it was to leap into the headlines once more at the end of the following year.

Meanwhile royal flying continued in several other directions. Among the six Rollason Turbulents, as the former French Durine design was now known, entered for the National Air Races in 1959, was the Tiger Club's G-APNZ. The entrant was the Duke of Edinburgh who, although familiar with the type in general and this individual example in particular as a pilot, had the machine flown for him on this occasion by his equerry, Squadron Leader John Severne who, in the 1960 King's Cup, was to achieve first place. Meanwhile the Queen's Flight was not idle and was involved in the visit to Nigeria of the Duke and Duchess of Gloucester. But despite such events as these the final year of the decade was a quiet one since, apart from the arrival of the royal helicopters, there seemed to be fewer worlds left to conquer and none of the contributions to aviation history were in the headline category. Also the aeronautical overtones of the Duke of Edinburgh's flight to India, Pakistan, Brunei and Sarawak at the beginning of the year were almost as lost on the general public, probably, as were those when the Queen Mother visited Kenya and Uganda a little later, or when the Duke flew to West Africa in the closing months. Even so, this is not to say that history was no longer capable of being made since even the latter trip achieved an interesting 'first', for, although it was now completely commonplace for members of the Royal Family to fly as passengers on Commonwealth tours, to embark on one such as a pilot was still unique. Inevitably it was Prince Philip who achieved this when, in November, he flew his own Heron to Accra from Hatfield at the beginning of his visit to Ghana.

The final month of the 1950s found the Duke back in Great Britain and paying a visit to the Royal Aircraft Establishment at Bedford. It was here that he had his first experience of not one but three automatic landings. The machine in which these were carried out was a Canberra and, with the Duke in the co-pilot's seat and Flight Lieutenant A.J. Camp as captain, the aircraft made a series of faultless landings at Thurleigh airfield in a cross-wind blowing at about 15 or more miles per hour. Perhaps it was a desire to get his hands back on the controls of a vehicle that prompted the Duke, only a few days later, to try flying a completely different machine when he took over a hovercraft of the SRN 1 type on the river Medina at Cowes.

The fascination that new eras seem to have for mankind, be they new year, fresh undertakings or just dates that end neatly with multiples of ten may be as commonly found among official bodies as with individuals. It is true that something of the sort prompted a long, hard look at the work of the Queen's Flight at the close of the decade and the conclusions were published in the aeronautical press. The review discovered that the Flight completed about 600 hours flying time annually and the greater part of this was carried out during the summer months. This is not to imply that the pilots were or are in any degree 'fair weather flyers', they rank among the most experienced pilots in the world, but just that the larger number of official engagements are carried out when the weather can be relied on to a greater extent. In addition to this was the fact that the machines flown by the flight were more suited to work within a range capability of 1,250 miles. Since the Heron Series 1 with fixed undercarriage had first appeared in 1950, and even the Series 2 which the Queen's Flight had always operated had a low cruising speed, these aircraft were now beginning to look decidedly 'elderly'. Meanwhile overseas commitments, of which there was a greater number during the winter, had continued to rely to a large extent on civil machines that were in regular service.

Enormous increases in civil air traffic over the United Kingdom had brought about a pressing need for increased safety regulations. While these were well able to cope with the increased tempo of air traffic over the country at this time, provision for the movement of royalty had to be slotted in. In order to simplify the situation, aircraft of the Royal Flight always flew in civil air corridors thus immediately placing themselves under civilian regulations, but now 'purple' airways were enforced in a vicinity of ten miles of any route taken over Great Britain. For journeys abroad, once diplomatic clearance had been obtained, it was a comparatively simple matter to follow the same procedures, particularly over member countries of the Commonwealth.

This pre-occupation with safety beyond the seemingly normal demands appeared to be justified by an event that took place towards the end of 1960 involving a Comet C2 with the Queen and Duke of Edinburgh as passengers. The aircraft in question was *Orion,* XK696, flown once again by Squadron Leader E.P. Pullan, the same officer who had flown Queen Elizabeth the Queen Mother and Princess Margaret to Rome the year before.

The Comet was flying in Airway Red One about 20 miles north-east of Eelde and at 35,000 feet in the Hanover FIR and, in fact, well on its way to bringing home the Queen and Duke from a trip to Denmark, where it had taken off from Copenhagen. The date was October 25. It was the co-pilot, Flight Lieutenant F.J. Stevens, who raised the alarm when he suddenly saw two jet fighters approaching on a collision course. There was no question as to their identity, they were North American F-86 Sabres of the West German Luftwaffe. Then, while those on board the royal air liner watched, the pair of fighters turned as one and banked over the Comet at a distance estimated as small as 50 feet. 'A very nasty moment', the pilot is reported to have commented later, 'I was prepared to do something drastic'.

Immediately after the incident, the two Sabres

Left *XM295 as it appeared before the application of trim to the cowlings* (de Havilland).

Right *The same aircraft showing the highly polished finish associated with royal machines before the application of the red scheme* (Crown Copyright).

were lost sight of but the matter did not rest there. Air Commodore Sir Edward Fielden, still Commander of the Queen's Flight was, as always, in the royal aircraft and is stated to have remarked 'The two aircraft had absolutely no business to be there', while perhaps recalling another incident of 'buzzing' by a fighter long years before when the Prince of Wales was his passenger.

Following the report of the incident events moved swiftly and an Anglo-German commission was immediately set up consisting of three Luftwaffe officers, Major G. Baumann, Lieutenant Colonel C. Cadow and Colonel H. Hauser, presided over by Group Captain I.J. Spencer, Commanding Officer of RAF Benson, assisted by Wing Commander P. Barker of RAF Transport Command. The incident also raised questions in the House of Commons the following day and in answer to a query the Air Minister, Mr George Ward, stated that already a draft agreement had been approved in principle on Eurocontrol.

At the resultant investigation the pilots of the F-86s stated that at all times the British machine had been in sight and in their opinion there had never been any danger of collision. The question was further complicated by the fact that the separation distance between the fighters and the transport was the subject of differing reports. In the light of this the British and German officials failed to reach an agreement on the wording of an announcement on the matter. A spokesman for the West German Defence Ministry, Colonel Gerd Schmueckle, said that a statement would be made public in two or three days but agreed that no further action would be called for from the German side—in fact the matter had been dropped since it was impossible to reach any firm conclusion.

An interesting and at first sight retrograde step was taken with regard to the Queen's Flight during that year when Her Majesty visited Nepal. In view of the fact that the royal Herons, which by this time had flown a total distance of over a million miles, had not the load carrying capacity over the mountainous regions, two Dakotas, KN452 and 645, were employed. Although there had been suggestions that the then-new Handley Page Herald was an alternative, this proposal was not taken up since the British aircraft was still far from fully proven.

When the Queen flew out to India at the start of her Asian tour she had done so in a Bristol Britannia but the veteran American types already there for her use proved each to have an interesting past, in that KN645 had once flown as the personal transport of Field Marshal Lord Montgomery, while KN452 had been the aircraft used for special duties in Malta by the AOC and it had only recently come from there.

Meanwhile the work of the Queen's Flight went ahead performing its often routine but necessary work. Queen Elizabeth the Queen Mother, who was bound by no such restrictions as were followed for her elder daughter's safety, namely never to travel in a single-engined aircraft, was by now something of a seasoned helicopter passenger and it was in a Westland Whirlwind that she flew to Devonport on March 14. On the deck of HMS *Ark Royal* waited a welcoming party including Vice Admiral Sir Charles Madden, C-in-C Plymouth Command, and it was on the flight deck of the carrier that the helicopter finally came to rest. It was Her Majesty's third visit to this vessel of which she was patron.

The same day found the Duke of Edinburgh at London Airport in his capacity of Grand Master of the Guild of Air Pilots and Air Navigators. With the chairman of BOAC he boarded a Boeing 707 belonging to the corporation. Some 70 of the other passengers were members of the Guild's Court and Livery, and included such distinguished members of the aviation world as Air Vice-Marshal Donald

Bennett, Captain O.P. Jones who, in earlier years had made his own contribution to royal flying, and Air Commodore Sir Frank Whittle. During the flight that followed, Prince Philip, who was travelling in the co-pilot's seat, took over the controls of the Boeing liner.

The Queen's Flight was still equipped in the main by the de Havilland Heron and the mid-summer of 1961 saw an extra one taken on charge in the form of a C2 model, XR391. In time it was joined in a new finish by the other machines on the strength. This was an overall coat of fluorescent red which, despite the addition of a broad blue cheat line, lost something of the crisp appeal of the former polished metal finish. Even so, as a safety measure, it was deemed to be justified but this use of high visibility red was in no way dictated by the near miss off Heligoland since that took place after the decision to adopt the scheme had been announced at the end of 1959.

During the year when the new finish had been adopted, another machine was added to the strength of the Flight. This was a trainer, a Chipmunk T10, and its finish was in accordance with the new scheme. The reason for the adoption of such an aircraft, which was to remain attached to Benson for the next three years, was that it was to be used for the flight instruction of Their Royal Highnesses Prince Michael, Prince Richard and the Duke of Kent.

For long range flights, Service machines from transport squadrons or civil aircraft continued to be used, not only for the Queen and Prince Philip but also for other members of the Royal Family. A typical case was that when Princess Margaret and Mr Anthony Armstrong-Jones (later Lord Snowdon) flew to Shannon on a scheduled service operated by a Viscount 808 aircraft. This was something of a minor historical milestone for it marked the first occasion when any member of the Royal Family had flown in the care of Aer Lingus and the couple made the return trip to England in a Boeing 720.

The year that followed was to see something of the end of an epoch, for, on January 1, Air Commodore Fielden, who had formed and moulded the formative years of what had been the King's Flight and re-established it and brought it to the prevailing peak of efficiency, was promoted to the rank of Air Vice-Marshal. He was also appointed Senior Air Equerry to the Queen and, in consequence, would retire from his former post as Extra Equerry and relinquish the command which he had established, namely that of Captain of the Queen's Flight. This was no retirement in the accepted sense, his promotion would bring with it many fresh responsibilities, but in a manner of speaking was a gesture of recognition after 33 years of devoted professional service. These changes created a vacancy for the first time for a new captain and Group Captain A.D. Mitchell, CVO, DFC and Bar, AFC, the former commander of RAF Cottesmore, was promoted to Air Commodore and assigned to the command. Under the new captain another change took place in the late summer of 1963 when the post of officer commanding was taken over by Wing Commander Anthony W. Ringer, AFC, who up to that time had been in charge of training at No 3 Group Headquarters. Previous to this he had been the liaison officer acting on behalf of Bomber Command with the firm of Handley Page at the time of the introduction of their Victor bomber into service and subsequently he had been in command of training connected with the new machine conducted from Gaydon.

In the years to come the Flight was to see other changes including at long last a replacement of the aging Heron machines.

Beyond the Seas

'I travelled among unknown men
In lands beyond the seas'
William Wordsworth

Historians are always blessed with the advantage of hindsight and from the vantage point of the present day it is easy to see the middle years of the 1960s as those of great change for the Queen's Flight. Not all of them were planned and one was of great tragedy, but the epoch began smoothly enough when, in the spring, new helicopters arrived. This new equipment was no more than a reflection of the general re-equipping that was taking place in the RAF and the first of the two new machines for royal use was taken over at Yeovilton on May 6 and flown to Benson.

The pair due for replacement had been powered by piston engines—radial, air-cooled motors giving 750 hp. The new version, on the other hand, was fitted with a Bristol Siddeley Gnome 101 turbo-shaft power unit rated at 1,050 shp. Still termed Whirlwinds, these were no more than the standard HC10 model with a few additional refinements to produce a special, or VVIP version, designated the HCC12. Their identities were XR486 and 487.

Meanwhile another change at Benson took the form of a disappearance, rather than a replacement, for the Chipmunk which had been on the strength of the Flight for over three years by this time was taken away. It had served its purpose well and three young men of the Royal Family, as described earlier, had all become familiar with the red-painted WP903, but now it was dismantled and placed in store with No 27 Maintenance Unit at RAF Shawbury.

By this time it had finally been decided to replace the elderly Heron aircraft. The type chosen was the Hawker Siddeley HS 748 Andover and the machines for royal service would be part of a batch of six supplied to the Royal Air Force. The Duke of Edinburgh was already familiar with the design having flown the civil demonstrator.

Andovers were in a sense jets but only in so much as their twin power plants were Rolls-Royce Dart R Da 7 Mk 532-2L turboprops, each rated at 2,290 shp. The first prototype had flown almost exactly four years earlier on June 24 1960 and the maiden flight of the first production machine had taken place on August 1 a year later. The concept of the design had been for a short and medium-range transport with a crew of two but the performance was better, giving a cruising speed in the region of 100 mph over that of the Herons.

Modifications to the new machines, of which there was to be a pair, at first included fitting out the interior with a cabin forward and an executive suite, although it was stated that conversion to other transport duties was possible in an emergency should this be called for. The first of these Andover CC2s was taken over on July 9 and the Heron earmarked for consequent disposal was that with the greatest total of flying hours, at the time, XH375. This had been taken on charge in May 1965, had since accumulated 3,560 hours and was disposed of in September, by which time all the aircraft of the Flight had been doped in the bright red finish. However this was never applied completely to the Andovers, the large prominent fin and rudder in a distinctive finish being regarded as sufficient. These machines were normally flown by an augmented crew of five, pilot, co-pilot, navigator and extra member, including the cabin attendant.

While the flight crews were becoming familiar with XS789, a second machine was being prepared and this, XS790, was to be delivered on August 7, six days after a new Captain of the Queen's Flight had taken up his duties, this being Air Commodore John H.L. Blount, DFC.

Continued use of aircraft from RAF transport squadrons or alternatively of civil machines was made throughout this period, whenever long distance flights were to be undertaken, and an example of the latter was to take place early in the following year when Her Majesty the Queen and the Duke of Edinburgh left for a state visit to Ethiopia on February 1. That this journey was of some small historical significance there is no doubt

Top left *Andover XS790 once more taxies past the Central Band of the Royal Air Force.* **Above left** *The same machine waits with a BBC tv camera and crew in the foreground.* **Above right** *The passenger on this occasion was HRH Prince Charles.*

since it marked the first occasion when the Queen, or indeed any other member of the Royal Family, was to fly in a VC10 aircraft. This was a civil example being BOAC's G-ARVL which took off at 7 am from London Airport in the hands of Captain A.S.M. Rendall, the VC10 flight manager, at the beginning of a journey of seven hours duration that was to cover 3,750 miles non-stop to Addis Ababa. The co-pilot on this occasion was Captain R.E. Knights.

A minor event of the month before had been the departure of another Heron, this time XM295, which had joined the Flight in April 1958 and by reason of its retention had now exceeded the total flying time of the previous machine by 150 hours. The remaining aircraft of this type were not to go until three years later.

February was also to see other royal journeys by air and one such using a borrowed Service transport was that undertaken by the Duke and Duchess of Kent. They had been flown to Gambia to take part in the celebrations to mark the Independence of the last of the former British colonies in Africa and XN404, a Bristol Britannia C2 named *Canopus,* was employed from the strength of No 511 Squadron to fly them out from Great Britain.

With the mixed equipment of Herons, Andovers and Whirlwind helicopters the work of the Queen's Flight continued throughout the next two years and more, so that the unit was 31 years old when next it came in for public attention. Alas, the means whereby it did so was also the first major accident in its history.

The date was December 7 1967 and one of the

Whirlwind helicopters, XR487, was on a journey from its base at Benson to the works of its builders, Westland, at Yeovil, Somerset. There were four occupants, the Captain of the Queen's Flight, Air Commodore J.H.L. Blount, the Engineering Officer of the Flight, Squadron Leader M.W. Hermon, the navigator, Flight Lieutenant R. Fisher and the pilot of the helicopter, Squadron Leader J.H. Liversidge. The aircraft was flying at an altitude of about 500 feet when watchers were astonished to see it suddenly plunge into the ground where it was totally wrecked, killing all on board. Shortly afterwards an official source described the incident as 'baffling' and it was certainly true that an on-the-spot examination of the immediate evidence indicated that a complete rotor blade had been lost while the helicopter was still in the air. Subsequent investigation revealed that, while the machine was passing over the village of Brightwalton in Berkshire, the rotor shaft had snapped. It was just one of those cases which do very occasionally happen in the world of aviation when, despite every care and precaution that men can devise, flying, so to speak, seems to bite the hand that guides it.

With John Blount's death in the service of his Queen a search began for a successor and at the end of January following, the announcement was made that a fresh appointment would take effect from the 15th of the month. The new Captain of the Queen's Flight was to be Air Commodore Archie L. Winskill, CBE, DFC and Bar, who had been born at Penrith in Cumberland and had served during the war years with distinction as a fighter pilot in both Great Britain and North Africa. His entry into the Royal Air Force had been made via the Volunteer Reserve in 1937 when he had trained as a pilot and it was not until three years later that he had been commissioned as a Pilot Officer. Following this, he flew with No 72 Squadron with Spitfire fighters from Gravesend in October 1940, having gained his first experience with these machines when with No 54 Squadron at an earlier date.

However, Pilot Officer Winskill's stay with the squadron in Kent was to last hardly a fortnight for, on October 17, he was posted to Hornchurch and Squadron Leader G.L. Denholm's No 603 Squadron, once more equipped with Spitfires.

The award of the first Distinguished Flying Cross came during the next year when serving with No 41 Squadron based at Catterick in 1941. During August he found himself engaged on escort duties over France. By this time his total flying hours had mounted to 250, all on operations and three Nazi aircraft had fallen to his guns. It was the same month that the work of escorting RAF bombers brought him one of his most spectacular engagements up to that time. Two Messerschmitt Bf 109s appeared unexpectedly and made a swift attack on the formation. He engaged the two so fiercely that both were driven off and one was claimed as a victory.

Such are the fortunes of aerial warfare that today's victor is tomorrow's victim and it was thus with Archie Winskill, for the same year found him shot down over occupied France. He subse-

Above right *The Herons lasted long enough to see the first introduction of red day-glo finish with blue trim.*

Right *The ill-fated XR487 which was lost in 1967, killing the Captain of The Queen's Flight.*

quently managed to escape to England after a difficult journey through Spain. Just before the opening of the North African campaign he was commanding No 232 Squadron, then preparing its Spitfires for the invasion of Algeria, and he continued to fly with this squadron until the end of the fighting in this theatre, the award of a Bar to his DFC being made during this period at the end of an extensive tour of Army close-support work.

By 1944 he was back in England once more and was chief instructor of the Fighting Wing of the Central Gunnery School but the following year was serving at the Air Ministry after graduation from the Army Staff College at Camberley, Surrey. Two years later he was abroad once more and again in command of a Spitfire squadron, this time No 17 based at Miho, Japan. In February, the squadron was disbanded there and as a result Air Commodore Winskill was appointed Air Adviser to the Belgian Government in 1949, a post which he held until going to study at the Joint Services Staff College in 1955.

Following the completion of this course he went to Edinburgh to take command of RAF Turnhouse and this appointment was not terminated until he returned once more to Europe where he worked on the staff of the 2nd Tactical Air Force in Germany in the operations and air plans section. His next posting was back in England when he assumed command of RAF Duxford, Cambridge, which, at that time, was still a fighter station. By now he had received the award of a CBE in 1960 and in the next year became Deputy Director of Personnel at the Air Ministry.

In 1964 Air Commodore Winskill was appointed British Air Attaché in Paris and he remained there until relinquishing the post in the summer of 1967 to join the Directorate of Public Relations in August. This was the appointment he held at the time of his selection to become Captain of the Queen's Flight and, despite the relatively short time that he had been in charge of Public Relations at the Air Ministry, there were those on his staff who remember their personal feelings of pleasure at his new work, to be tinged with a feeling of regret at the loss of an officer who had made himself so popular among those under him.

There were other changes about to take place in the Queen's Flight at this period, not only among personal appointments but also concerning the equipment. Perhaps the most important of these was the disposal of the last pair of de Havilland Herons. XR391, the more recent acquisition had a comparatively low total of flying hours, standing at exactly 1,820 when it was disposed of just seven years after having joined the Flight, in June, when it passed to the Royal Navy. The other Heron, XM296, which had been taken on the strength of the Flight in April 1958, was likewise pensioned off with a total of 4,310 hours, the largest of any of the four, during July. This was taken over by the Air Officer Commander in Chief, Germany, who retained it until 1972.

It might not be irrelevant to digress briefly at this point to trace the subsequent history of a representative aircraft such as this, if only as an illustration of the economies which are practised as a matter of course. This aircraft, which had been originally built by the parent company at Hatfield, was by no means at the end of its career when it ceased to be used by its second 'owners' in the last decade for, immediately after this had been relegated from use by the AOC-in-C, it passed to No 781 Squadron RNAS at Lee-on-Solent. Its service here was comparatively brief, for its standards of comfort and reliability were not long unrecognised and a subsequent transfer found it at the disposal of the Flag Officer Naval Air Command and based at HMS *Heron,* otherwise RNAS Yeovilton, where this 'personal barge' was the subject of a light-hearted coming of age ceremony in 1979. Its appearance is little changed from the days of its royal service and

A de Havilland Heron is guided in by a 'batsman' (Crown Copyright).

it is maintained in a smart polished metal and white finish, relieved only by the naval flags of rank below the flight deck and the broad green cheat line and lettering above the windows.

Two other changes were to take place in the Queen's Flight in 1968, the first of these being to take on charge a fresh Andover transport. This was XS793, another of the half dozen originally built for RAF use and was added to the group at Benson to replace the two Herons. The lost helicopter in which the four officers died had also to be replaced but it was not possible to furnish one to VVIP standards immediately; as a substitute, therefore, a standard Westland Whirlwind HAR10, XP299, was delivered in camouflage finish, on temporary loan.

The reason for a permanent replacement not being found was partly revealed earlier in the year by the announcement that plans were well advanced to adopt Wessex helicopters as soon as possible. The Under Secretary of State for Defence had been at pains to make it clear in the Commons on February 22 that the replacement decision was in no way a 'panic' one dictated by the loss of the Whirlwind earlier, but had been finally taken some time prior to the tragedy.

As the summer of 1968 advanced there were other plans afoot in the Royal Family with regard to aviation and the immediate result of one was the order to extract from store at Shawbury the Chipmunk trainer there, WP903. The reason for this was that it had been decided to give Prince Charles some air experience in a machine of this type to discover if he had any aptitude for flying. That the series of trips began on Tuesday, July 30 showed he had, is hardly surprising. His father had been a pilot with a large number of types in his logbook as long as the younger man could remember and he had always shown the family characteristic of preferring to participate rather than just watch. The pilot on the occasion of these tests, which lasted for several days, was Squadron Leader Philip Pinney, one of the instructors of the Central Flying School and the flights were carried out from RAF Tangmere, the former Battle of Britain fighter station. There was no doubt as to the aptitude of the Prince and flying lessons were begun, still using the Chipmunk. The culmination which crowns every pilot's ambition arrived on January 14 the following year when the instructor suddenly climbed down and told his pupil he was on his own, and the Prince of Wales made his first solo at Bassingbourn. The successful completion of this preliminary training was marked by two presentations, one from the ground crew who had been responsible for the care of the machine he had used. This took the form of a model of the aircraft mounted on an inscribed plinth; the other recognition of this milestone in every flyer's career took place back at Tangmere on August 2 when the AOC-in-C handed over the 80-hour qualification award.

At much the same time other members of the Royal Family were passing different aviation milestones. For the Duke of Edinburgh one of these was the entry of the 49th type in his logbook. The design in question was the Short Skyvan which he flew at Benson for a total time of 45 minutes making three landings and take-offs in the company of the firm's chief test pilot, Don Wright.

Princess Margaret, too, was noting a significant stage in aeronautical development, not in the air but on the ground and in Tokyo, for it was here on the Smith's Industries stand at the British Exhibition that she was able to see at first hand the latest head-up display equipment. Meanwhile Lord Louis Mountbatten was flying with Sir Alec Douglas Home from London Airport to attend the funeral of President Eisenhower.

These were among the great events of royal aviation in 1969, or at least those which were regarded as worthy of note by the press, technical and popular, but there were others. Reading history at Trinity College, Cambridge, the Prince of Wales had continued his flying training and a Beagle Basset was soon to be seen at RAF Oakhampton and later Benson for his use in converting to twin-motored aircraft, still in the care of Philip Pinny. Although the photographs taken to mark His Highness' 21st birthday were a little premature since they showed him at the controls of such a type, in fact he was not to solo with a 'twin' until the next year, on February 13. When the day arrived the flight was made with a navigator on board; not that this was in any way similar to the events surrounding his grandfather's solo, but an adherence to the prevailing normal RAF multi-conversion policy.

This event had caused little stir among the media and still less was stimulated by the earlier visit to South America carried out with the aid of a VC10 machine by Her Majesty the Queen, so common-place now was royal air travel, yet strangely the event that marked the end of a long saga of devoted skill was to pass almost unnoticed by the majority.

For the greater part of eight years now, as earlier recorded, Air Vice-Marshal Sir Edward Hedley Fielden, GCVO, CB, DFC, AFC of Pangbourne, near Reading, Berks, had performed the duties of Senior Air Equerry but now it was announced he would be finally retiring at the end of the year. He had been responsible for all the royal air journeys, not only those in the earliest days of the 'Royal Flight' but also throughout the whole of the reign of

This page top *Pilot Princes. The Duke of Edinburgh leaves Viking VL246 at Wattisham and* **Bottom** *Prince Charles in the cockpit of the red Chipmunk WP903 during flight training* (Crown Copyright).

Right *Sailors both. HRH Prince Philip talks to ex-RNAS pilot J. Parkinson (centre)* (Crown Copyright).

the Queen's father and he was to see the small organisation blossom to become an established and highly-efficient part of Transport Command. So lengthy had been his service that he had seen the adoption of Herons to replace the post-war Vikings and even the former give way to Andovers. But probably more momentous than any up-grading of aircraft types was the introduction of helicopters with the small beginnings of a mail carrier until the present recognised use of that type of aircraft is such that the establishment of the Queen's Flight now always includes an officer of the Royal Navy to act as pilot of one.

The man to achieve what amounts to the creation in practical working service terms of something completely new, Edward Fielden, who additionally held the French Croix de Guerre in recognition of his wartime work in connection with 'moonlight missions', had been born in 1903. The nick-name 'Mouse', on account of his retiring nature, was nowhere more appreciated than at Buckingham Palace and elsewhere so that the school-boy appelation remained throughout his life.

More than this, his 'unflappable' nature, coupled with a great flair for organisation, made him eminently suitable for the work. An early example of this was the occasion, years earlier when, with Prince Edward and Hugh Mellor, he was forced to make an emergency landing that broke the plane's axle. Shaken although the two were, their concern was all the greater at the realisation of the possible narrow escape of their illustrious passenger who, in point of fact, almost seemed to be enjoying the whole escapade. Fielden, always quickly master of any situation, remembered that it was only necessary to find some means of supplying the Prince with a cup of tea and a charged pot to pour more from. So he straight-away found a small house where the lady within was able to find the necessary beverage, and 'Mouse' was then able to begin the necessary moves for their rescue, secure in the knowledge that his simple strategem was catering for his charge's comfort.

Yet to describe Edward Fielden in terms like this alone paints an incomplete picture which fails to do him justice since he was, moreover, a very experienced airman. A friend over many years recalls the way in which this was concealed in the manner common to many flying officers, namely by a deceptively light-hearted style coupled with a highly developed sense of fun and an ability to appreciate the good things in life.

All this could be, and often was, hidden beneath a certain urbanity of exterior which seemed incapable of descending to stiff and meaningless formality for, whatever the occasion, his graceful good manners,

untinged by pedantry, always shone through so that his work seemed almost to be in the nature of the lightest, a characteristic not uncommon either then or now among the senior members of the royal household, so that the work of their colleagues is made easier and seemingly lighter.

Her Majesty the Queen liked Sir Edward Fielden tremendously, not only for the qualities already outlined but because he epitomised the ability, that still continues in her Flight, to discharge any duty that came its way for members of the family, its staff, government ministers and visiting dignitaries with an efficiency that was unvarying, for Fielden was over all the completely competent professional who loved the work he was doing. For the role of Captain of the Queen's Fight that he established was not only a job calling for airmanship and skill as a courier alone, when actually flying with the Queen's person in his care, it also called on great technical ability and endurance even at the planning stage. Any series of royal journeys calling for continuous flights in a wide spectrum of climes often demanded considerable work on 'proving runs' when not only had times to be checked, fuel facilities to be assured and calculations to be confirmed, but also aerodromes had to be tested and every detail examined in the light of prevailing demands,

political climates abroad and the royal itinerary: in short overseeing every stage of all the flights. Now, with the end of the decade fading on the last day of the old year all this, and the duties he had performed of late as Senior Air Equerry, were at an end: in later years the distinguished BBC Court Correspondent, Godfrey Talbot, was to sum up the qualities of Sir Edward Fielden succinctly as 'A rare spirit, marvellous companion and host . . .'.

When 1970 began to be written on the datelines of the world it was not to indicate any great change in either the equipment or the command of the Flight, although the different tradesmen came and went with their tours of duty, and the machines still stood at no more than the three Hawker Siddeley Andovers and the pair of Westland Wessex helicopters plus Prince Charles' Beagle B206 Basset. The historic Chipmunk WP903 was back at Shawbury and in the care of No 27 Maintenance Unit again and was to languish there for four years until it was offered for sale in March 1974 to be purchased finally on the strength of its new civil registration, G-BCGC, by the Culdrose Gliding Club which reckoned that it bore the initials of that organisation. But perhaps the chief event of the home year at Benson was the visit paid to the Flight in February by the Chief of Air Staff, Air Chief Marshal Sir John Grandy, GCB, KBE, DSO, accompanied by Lady Grandy. On their arrival they were greeted by Air Commodore Winskill, Captain of the Flight, and by Wing Commander M.J. Rayson, the Commanding Officer. The tour covered all aspects of the work accomplished by the unit including the engineering section under the care of Squadron Leader J. Marshall, via the Helicopter Support Section, to such relatively unsung but necessary departments as the Mechanical Transport Section and the colourful Flag Store, with its banners, standards and ensigns. But work on preparations for visits such as this was among the high spots of an arduous timetable for, although not involved in terms of aircraft, the experience and organisational skills of the Flight were placed at the disposal of other Commonwealth countries from time to time and 1970 was no exception. This was the year of the Queen's visit to Australia and, on this occasion, the aircraft and crews were found by the Royal Australian Air Force. Chief among the machines which featured were the BAC One-Eleven and the Hawker-Siddeley HS-748, both from No 34 Squadron, and

Above left *DHC1 Chipmunk WP903 now in red finish and used as a trainer by Prince Charles* (Crown Copyright).

Left *The Prince of Wales inspects the rotor head of a Naval Wessex helicopter* (RNAS Yeovilton).

Prince Andrew on receipt of his parachute wings. Two Royal Marine Commandos are receiving similar awards (RAF News).

April found the crews kept busy on a number of trips mainly in New South Wales.

A little under a year later it was announced that the Prince of Wales would be joining the first graduate entry at the RAF College, Cranwell. This consisted entirely of post-graduates who had also undergone some training on preliminary aircraft and the instruction for advanced students was scheduled to be continued on Jet Provosts. With his 80-hour experience, the Prince fell into this category as was obvious from the fact that he flew himself to the Lincolnshire College in his own Beagle Basset. Dual experience was to be supervised by Squadron Leader R.E. Johns who was also to oversee the ground syllabus which included on a tutorial basis airmanship, aerodynamics, meteorology, navigation, medicine and survival.

The summer was to bring new aviation adventures for the Royal Family in general and for Prince Charles in particular, who was granted no quick path to the achievement of wearing RAF wings. Although spinning for prolonged periods made him feel unwell, nevertheless problems such as these were overcome as much by the Prince's iron determination as by the skill and refusal to be daunted by the task exhibited by 'Dick' Johns, for the immediate responsibility for the survival of any young man is an awesome enough prospect, now magnified by the close attention paid to seemingly every detail of the Prince's progress by the media.

A case in point was that when some astute reporters on the staff of a popular newspaper noted a remark made on television which seemed to indicate that the Jet Provost used for the Prince's instruction had been specially modified to improve its performance at altitude and a series of telephone calls to the Ministry of Defence at once ensued. But what was revealed was not that the machine had any changes of this sort, but that it was one of several that had them and that there was a programme to include progressively the changes throughout the range of trainers. In this particular case the sharpness of the perception shown by the representatives of the Press had performed a service for it is certain that many other people also jumped to an incorrect assumption based on an ambiguous reference to factory inspection procedure, but it is also an example of the strength of the publicity in the light of which the pupil had to learn and the instructor to teach, factors that are absent from flying training usually.

Another facet of the Prince of Wales' keen interest in aviation that was flung open to public gaze a few months later was the occasion when he elected to make a parachute jump from an Andover of the normal Service pattern flying at 1,200 feet above the sea near the Dorset coast. Jumps such as this are not part of the RAF's regular course of instruction and the idea came from the Prince himself. The day in question was July 28 and even the preparations for the jump when Prince Charles drew a couple of parachutes from store were carried out in front of a group of press cameras.

Interest in the drop was only to be expected—it was the first time in history that an heir to the throne had jumped out of an aeroplane—but the attention it received seems unlikely to have contributed much to pre-flight calm for the unfortunate principal performer. An unexpected turn of events took place at the moment following that when the Prince stepped into space for instead of dropping away in the textbook manner he was whirled over with his feet in the rigging lines. Luckily they failed to become entangled and matters righted themselves for a landing to be made in the sea from which a plastic in-shore rescue boat plucked the Prince in a matter of seconds; but the explanation came later from Prince Charles himself. 'Hollow legs', he said.

A little less than a month later, on August 20, the benefit of attending Cranwell and thus having a chance to concentrate on flying training rather than fit it in with other commitments, as had been the lot

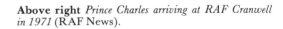

Left *Prince Charles and Prince Andrew together undergo parachute instruction* (RAF News).

Below left *The Prince of Wales in full parachute rig* (RAF News).

Above right *Prince Charles arriving at RAF Cranwell in 1971* (RAF News).

Right *A royal Andover but not part of the Flight. Here XS794 of the former Transport Command has just landed with HRH Princess Alexandra who is being greeted at the foot of the steps* (Crown Copyright).

of previous royal gentlemen, paid off at a ceremony at the college when the Prince received his wings from the Chief of Air Staff, Sir Denis Spotswood. That they had been well and truly earned there is no question for not only had the young man gained new and undemanded experience in the flight from Abingdon for the parachute jump but he had put in time aboard a Hawker Siddeley Nimrod on July 21 during a flight from Kinloss.

Although the spotlight of publicity had played for so long on the aeronautical activities of Prince Charles, it would be entirely wrong to assume that other members of the Royal Family at the same time had lost their appetite for aviation outside the line of duty. History continued to be made by the Duke of Edinburgh, not only in a mild way such as during the trip when he had been flown by his son for the first time in a machine attached to the Queen's Flight but also in such major fields as a journey in the supersonic Concorde airliner, thus carrying on the same ideas which had prompted the Comet flights of 20 years before. The date of this latter event was January 12 1972 and for a period of about one and a half hours, the Duke had taken the controls of 002 at Mach 2 over the Bay of Biscay at an altitude of 50,000 feet.

The role of the Queen's Flight continued unchanged and necessary into the 1970s. Perhaps because it had first been conceived in a democratic country with a constitutional monarchy this arrangement was still the best and capable of very little in the way of alteration or improvement. The use made of the facilities of the Flight by others outside the Royal Family in the execution of their official duties continued, as had been the way since the formation of the unit, and the early 1970s were no different nor is that role changed today. To list the commitments carried out by ministers of the crown that call for swift, unobtrusive yet efficient transportation by air would be wearisome but it is probably sufficient to cite a case in point for the beginning of the decade and state that even Britain's membership of the Common Market was ushered in with the aid of the Flight. For it was in one of the Andovers, XS793, that the Prime Minister was flown to Brussels on January 22 1972 in order that he might sign the agreement binding Britain to the EEC. Visiting heads of state, including royalty, also make use of the 'royal airline'.

On the other side of the proverbial coin, the Royal Family continued to make use of aircraft to carry out some of their multitude of duties abroad and the custom continued of flying in Royal Air Force machines when the occasion demanded,

mainly drawn from No 216 Squadron which had very much assumed the same importance in this capacity as had been enjoyed earlier in No 24 (Communications) Squadron. They still flew later versions of the Comet and it was in one of these that Princess Alexandra and her husband, the Honourable Angus Ogilvy, flew to the Far East and Afghanistan that year. In so doing they supplied the popular press with one of their most widely-used photographs when the couple posed for cameramen with the flight crew and cabin staff.

However, the year was to have other bearings on the history of the Queen's Flight which were to close an era begun with the first flight of an adventurous young prince, 54 years previously. May found the Queen and Prince Philip once more following the pattern set by 'Edward the Peacemaker' in another age and at the conclusion of another series of visits abroad. While coming home the couple broke their journey in France where they paid a visit on the Queen's uncle, the Duke of Windsor, at his home in the Bois de Boulogne. Unfortunately His Highness was in frail health and although the visit brought him much joy it was not possible for him to see off the Queen and Duke so that the leave-taking on the doorstep was attended by the Duchess. On May 28, Prince Edward, Duke of Windsor, died at his home from cancer of the throat.

His body was to be flown to England on the Wednesday following accompanied by the Duchess, but at the last minute it was announced that Her Grace was too unwell to make the journey immediately. Thus it was that no widow accompanied the Duke's remains when they were flown home on a bright and windy morning in a Royal Air Force VC10. Even in death royalty must exhibit the 'courtesy of princes' and be punctual and the transport machine with its sad burden was to be seen circling Benson for a short while before touching down. As the aircraft rolled to a stop and the Guard of Honour found by the Queen's Colour Squadron came to attention the bearer party moved forward and the doors of the VC10 opened.

There exist standing orders on the procedure to be adopted by the RAF when a member of the Royal Family dies abroad and they were followed now. Slowly the group of hatless officers took the weight of the coffin and bore it with measured tread towards the little mortuary chapel of RAF Benson, their gloves making a splash of white across the shoulders of their fellows to relieve the over-all pattern of blue-grey. As they passed along, the wind over the Oxfordshire countryside made the trees dip and sway so that an elderly lady witness, who could recall the dead Duke as a golden-haired young Prince, was moved to remark 'Even the trees are bowing to the old king'.

At 7 am the following morning the coffin, having been guarded all night by a vigil of officers, with reversed arms at each corner of the catafalque, was taken by road to Windsor for the public lying in state. On the following Friday the Duchess of Windsor arrived in England in an Andover of the Queen's Flight which landed at London Airport to a small welcoming party, led by Admiral of the Fleet Earl Mountbatten of Burma.

The funeral of the Duke took place on Monday, June 5, and the day after, the Duchess was to depart once more from Heathrow. She was escorted to the airport by the Lord Chamberlain and a member of the royal household was to accompany her on the flight back to France. Once more an Andover stood ready on the tarmac and those gathered nearby saw a small, trim figure, clad in black, mount the aircraft steps and vanish inside without a backward glance. The door was closed, the throttles were pushed forward and the machine slowly taxied out to await clearance. There was a short wait before the Andover was away, and quickly became no more than a silhouette against the June sky. The Flight had served, for the last time, the man who had created it in taking his widow home.

* * * * *

Below left *One of the new Andover machines was delivered in August 1964. XS790 is shown here* (Hawker Siddeley).

Right *The Prince of Wales before completion of his training as a pilot with the AOC-in-C (left) at Cranwell during 1971* (Crown Copyright).

For Her Majesty the Queen also, the year was something of a special one from the aeronautical angle, although it must have had overtones of deep family sadness, for it was on Wednesday, November 15, that she opened, at long last, the Royal Air Force Museum at Hendon, the same museum of which her husband had been patron from its formative years. Unfortunately he was not able to be present on the opening day due to commitments abroad but it was not long after his return to Great Britain that the Duke was conducted round the exhibits by the Museum's Keeper of Aircraft and Records, Mr J.M. Bruce.

The other probable absence from the ceremony was brought about by the death in a flying accident on Monday, August 28, of His Royal Highness, Prince William of Gloucester, who had begun his pilot training in 1960 in the Chipmunk. Two years later he could claim 60 hours' experience as a pilot after being a member of the University Air Squadron while he was at Cambridge but he added nothing to this until business took him to Africa where he joined the Lagos Flying Club. It was largely due to his active participation in the events of this organisation which prompted him to purchase a Piper Twin Comanche which he flew, not only out to Nigeria but also on the journey via the Sudan, brought about by his appointment to the British Embassy in Tokyo. In 1971 he won seventh place in the King's Cup among 27 entrants and at the same time became the first royal entrant to fly in the contest himself.

Prince William's death took place with dramatic suddeness at the start of a flight from Halfpenny Green which marked the start of the Goodyear Trophy Air Race. The weather was good but about half a minute after take-off, at exactly 3.32 pm, the Piper Cherokee Arrow 200, G-AYPW, appeared to bank fairly sharply to port and crash after the wing tip struck a tree. Also killed in the crash was his friend, Lieutenant Commander Vyrell Mitchell, with whom the Prince had participated in a number of air races and who had accompanied him on the Tokyo excursion.

Perhaps the shadow of memories such as these were not far from the minds of the gathering at Hendon in the middle of November that year. At this ceremony when Her Majesty unveiled a plaque over the main staircase in the entrance foyer, she was welcomed by a party including Lord Carrington, Secretary of State for Defence, the same Chief of Air Staff who had presented Prince Charles with his pilots brevet; Marshal of the Royal Air Force Sir Dermot Boyle, chairman of the trustees; and Dr John Tanner, the Director, who, with Sir Dermot, had done so much and over such a protracted period to bring the idea of a Royal Air Force Museum to practical realisation.

Before touring the museum with Dr Tanner as guide, the Queen's speech made mention of the facts that the RAF had been formed in the time of her grandfather and that her father, uncles, husband and eldest son were all officers of the same Service. It seemed a fitting conclusion to a chapter in the history of the Royal Family and the art of flying which, as we have seen, may be traced back before even the idea of a royal flight, anticipating even that forerunner of the RAF, the Royal Flying Corps, when aerial armies thought in terms of the gas balloon. However, tomorrow's progress becomes yesterday's history and the future still held some secrets for flying and the Queen's Flight.

A Newer World

'Tis not too late to seek a newer world . . .
Though much is taken, much remains'
Alfred, Lord Tennyson

The pattern of British aviation and its connections with the Royal Family continued largely unchanged into the first quarter of the last decade with the regular use of the aeroplane for the performance of the vast spectrum of responsibilities which could only widen as the world in part assumed a greater lowering of its barriers, and the aeroplane helped to save time for even short distance travel within the United Kingdom. An example as good as any other of this may be found in the period of the trip by Wessex helicopter made by Princess Alexandra, the Honourable Mrs Angus Ogilvy, to the RAF hospital at Wroughton in 1973, the same year that saw Princess Anne experience with her fiancé, Captain Mark Phillips, supersonic flight at Mach 2 for a period of some 20 minutes in Concorde 002 before it landed at Fairford.

But this was the era of the helicopter, the mode of transport which really owed its introduction for royal work to the Duke of Edinburgh when he began to use one to get quickly in and out of the grounds of Buckingham Palace to avoid the build-up of London traffic. By now his skill in this field of piloting had been passed on to his eldest son who carried out his first solo at RNAS Yeovilton in a Wessex 5 of No 707 Squadron of the Fleet Air Arm. It was in the same type that His Royal Highness led the flypast at the end of the helicopter course there in September 1974, the same Prince who, as a very small boy had stood with his parents and family on the balcony of Buckingham Palace overlooking The Mall and stared upward at the mass flypast mounted to mark his mother's Coronation one wet afternoon in 1953.

Yet except in memory, time never stands still and the dictates of economy affect us all so that the price of progress is all too often the abandonment of the long-lasting and the trusty. It was in something of this type of atmosphere that the decision was made to disband No 216 Squadron of the Royal Air Force, the fateful day being June 27 1974 at Lyneham. Throughout the history of any Service there are always the periods when units vanish but the loss of this one was of some historical significance because, like No 24 Squadron before it, 'Two-Sixteen' as it was commonly known, held something of a unique position in the annals of the Service. For once the Comets were received, not only royalty, but also many eminent visitors from all over the world, had been passengers in the immaculate jets. For this type of work the internal arrangements were specially conceived in such a manner that each section was separate, including the office and staff quarters.

The precedent for the special role of 'Two-Sixteen' had been set as far back as 1959 when the announcement was made in the Commons during April that, in future, the longer journeys undertaken by the Royal Family and distinguished persons would be made in Comets of Transport Command. The time that had followed was one in which the sleek and efficient shape of these machines had demanded attention throughout the world and must, at the same time, have added prestige to the British aircraft industry and to the Royal Air Force, an important factor that is too often overlooked by commentators.

Despite these privileges, the squadron was in no way an élite or special one, but an integral part of Transport Command, although it did have the honour of giving Her Majesty the Queen her first experience of jet flight and, after that day in 1957, it flew many members of the Royal Family. One of the last was Princess Alexandra who arrived at London Airport one night after performing the opening ceremony of the British Trade Fair in Sao Paulo while the winding up of the squadron was being planned—a victim of the current round of defence cuts. Nevertheless there still lies in the preserved archives of No 216 Squadron, a flimsy sheet of white paper in a buff envelope. It is a telegram from Her Majesty the Queen dispatched on the afternoon before the last day of the unit's official existence, thanking the squadron for their service over the years when they flew Comet aircraft.

That the relationship between the world of aviation and the Royal Family was something unique and to be cherished by the nation was given one of its rare public displays in the early spring of 1977 when the decision was taken at the Royal Air Force Museum to mount an exhibition expressing this special state of affairs. In their search for completeness, the organisers had cast their net widely, not only over the present but back along extensive corridors of years so that the display included a letter to George III from the Italian balloonist, Vincenzo Lunardi, the same Prince from Naples who made the first balloon flight in England where he was his country's ambassador in 1784.

Perhaps among the more personal relics were the uniforms worn by royal flyers and, as a strange mixture of the older ways of the world with modern technology, a sword received on the occasion of the first commercial flight of the Concorde from the Emir of Bahrein by His Royal Highness the Duke of Kent. The reason for the choice of date for this unique display was to mark the Silver Jubilee of Queen Elizabeth II and, among the aeronautical curios on show, was a memento from an earlier Silver Jubilee, that of Her Majesty's grandfather, King George V. This was the stone plaque from Mildenhall commemorating the earlier Royal Review of the Royal Air Force at Mildenhall which had survived there until removed to appear under the lights in London, a slab of weathering stone alongside the models of so many of the earlier aircraft of the King's Flight which for years had graced the offices of Sir Edward Fielden.

As with the past, so with the present, and as was only right and proper the Royal Air Force was once more reviewed by the Sovereign in 1977. This time the ceremonies took place at RAF Finningley in South Yorkshire and at the same time the Royal Air Force in the United Kingdom was presented with a new Colour by the Queen.

The first part of the review took the form of an inspection of a vast static display of machines representing all the current types in service and, to carry out this part of the review, Her Majesty drove between twin ranks of Service aircraft ranging from Jaguar fighters of Anglo-French design to

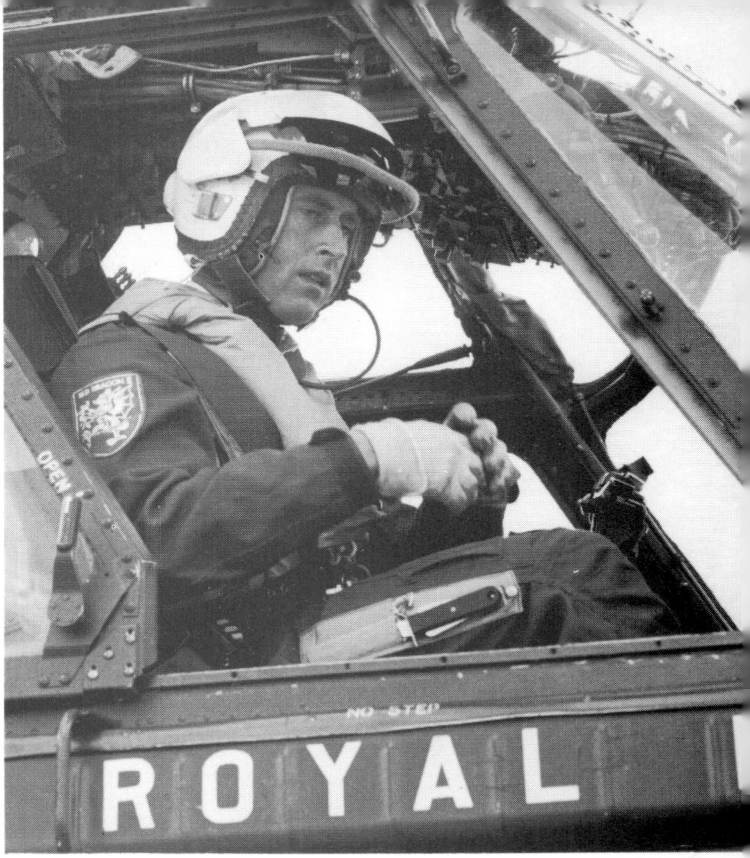

Above right *Prince Charles aboard a Naval Wessex helicopter in 1974. Note the Cadwallader badge on his overalls.*

Right *HM the Queen at the Royal Review of the RAF, held at Finningley in July 1977, where aircraft from 13 stations were on view* (RAF News).

This page above left *The Queen talks to Commonwealth Officers during the Silver Jubilee Review at RAF Finningley* (RAF News). **Above** *During the 1977 Royal Review, the Queen presented new Colours to the Royal Air Force in the United Kingdom. This was also the first occasion when all the Service's Colours and Standards were paraded simultaneously* (RAF News). **Left** *Accompanied by the Chief of Air Staff, Air Marshal Sir Michael Beetham GCB, CBE, DFC, AFC, ADC, the Queen is shown the main rotor gearbox of a Whirlwind helicopter at RAF Finningley. The following month she was to have her first experience of rotary wing flight when she visited Northern Ireland in XV732 on August 10/11* (RAF News).

Above right *The Prince of Wales in a Buccaneer at Yeovilton before flying to HMS* Ark Royal *in September 1977* (RNAS Yeovilton). **Right** *Comets of Air Support Command's No 216 Squadron were traditionally associated with providing long-distance transport for the Royal Family since 1959 when it was part of Transport Command. One such machine is seen here as Her Majesty begins an inspection* (RAF News).

Bloodhound surface-to-air missiles. All squadrons currently in existence were represented and, in order to permit this, a single type from each was displayed. Despite the title of the parade there were also representatives of the Commonwealth air forces of Canada, Australia and New Zealand in addition to the Central Flying School, Central Gliding School, Queen's University Air Squadron and the Air Experience Flight. The display part of the programme was repeated on the day following that on which the Queen attended, Friday, July 29, with the result that approaching 200,000 people saw more than 200 aircraft.

In order to reduce the time taken by the warplanes to fly over they did so in representative formations such as that mounted to stand for work over oceans, consisting of Buccaneers, Nimrods and Phantoms. Since reviews of this sort are intended to reflect the work of a complete Service there was also a group from the fighter squadrons and another consisting of Hercules transports. Trainers, too, were part of the flypast with Dominies and Jetstreams. Despite this display of might, the machine which in a sense stole the show and was undoubtedly noted by Her Majesty was the first of 15 Vickers-Slingsby T61E Venture motor gliders for the instruction of cadet gliding schools, a striking little aeroplane among the 70 on static display.

The extent to which things had changed in the Royal Air Force was emphasised by the mounting of a take-off by Vulcan bombers for this was the day when bombers and not fighters were sent climbing into the blue at only minutes notices. But although the wave of excitement, as far as the general public was concerned, had now passed to the bombers of Strike Command, the fighters were not to be outdone. No doubt, the exhibition that lingered longest in the mind, of the many feats performed that July day, was that when an F-111 of the Royal Australian Air Force took the aerial stage. With the nose well up into an almost vertical climb the pilot brought a gasp from the assembled spectators by the simple expedient of switching on both the fuel jettison and afterburner simultaneously with the resultant flame springing back behind the hurtling fighter for a distance greater than its own length.

The afternoon also presented a facet of the standards to which training can be taken in the Service and to do this there could be no better choice than one of the immaculately polished presentations from the cream of the world's aerobatic team, the Red Arrows, who were not satisfied with the well-loved programme alone, but introduced a new item to mark the year, the Jubilee Break.

Yet to paint a picture that is anything like

Left *The crew of the first Australian aircraft to carry the Queen, a BAC-111, on April 2 1970* (RAAF).

Below right *The RAF about to mount guard at Buckingham Palace to mark their Jubilee. The Queen's Colour of the RAF in the UK is being paraded* (Crown Copyright).

complete of an air force or any Service, its traditions must be remembered and this had, in part, been done a little earlier when the standards were paraded. Now it was the turn of the surviving aircraft of an earlier day and across the airfield came the once familiar sound of Merlin engines as the RAF Battle of Britain Memorial Flight displayed a Hawker Hurricane, a Vickers Supermarine Spitfire and an Avro Lancaster bomber. Euroworld's Boeing B-17, which dropped a parachute team, provided a moment of recollection of the three squadrons which had once flown the type in British colours, although the survivor on this occasion retained its United States insignia. Yet this was no review devoted to a maudlin glance over the shoulder, for the present was brought forcibly home by the array of missiles and by the sound as of tearing cloth as a Tornado fighter rent the heavens with its flypast so that there was no doubt that the Finningley review was in truth, 'fit for a Queen'.

It was no more than coincidence that this occasion took place in the year it did for, as is the way of Jubilee celebrations, the Commonwealth had been paid several visits in various parts a little earlier, all of these excursions calling in some measure for travel by air. Eight different types of machine had been involved taking Her Majesty the Queen and the Duke of Edinburgh a total distance of only a little under 31,000 miles round the earth and ten different airlines had participated when the couple landed back at London Airport on March 31 after a tour which had begun on February 9 and embraced Australia, Papua, New Guinea, New Zealand, the Pacific area and several of the associated islands.

The Queen was once more with her airmen the following year which marked the 60th anniversary of the formation of the Royal Air Force and, at 11 am on Saturday, April 1 1978, a service of thanksgiving and commemoration was held at Westminster Abbey with Her Majesty and other members of the Royal Family in attendance.

They were preceded by the Lord Mayor of Westminster who was received by the Dean and Chapter at the Great West Door at 10.52 am and conducted to his seat in the Quire. Three minutes later, Her Royal Highness the Princess Margaret, Countess of Snowdon, was received at the same spot before the arrival of the Queen and His Royal Highness Prince Philip, Duke of Edinburgh, who arrived at 10.57 am and were conducted into the Abbey by the umbrella party, paraded with the guard of honour, for April was coming in with its usual caprices of weather. As the hands of nearby Big Ben moved to 11 Her Majesty and their Royal Highnesses, together with the Collegiate Body and Preacher, moved in procession from the West End of the Abbey into the Quire by way of the South Aisle while the processional hymn, No 256, was being sung.

When all were in their places, the Queen's Colour for the Royal Air Force in the United Kingdom and that for the Royal Air Force, Germany, were borne from the Chapel of St George to the steps of the Sacrarium by Flying Officer D.R.E. Evans and Flight Lieutenant R.S. Booth, with

Sergeant C. Woodmansey and Sergeant L.D. Mailey acting as escorts to the Colours with Warrant Officers D.G. Strudwick and A. Mason bringing up the rear as Colour Warrant Officers. Here they were received by the Precentor and the Chaplain of Westminster Abbey who delivered the Colours to the Dean who, before a fanfare of trumpets was sounded, laid them on the High Altar.

During the service that followed the playing of the national anthem, the Oration by Pericles which ends with the words '. . . freedom is the sure possession of those alone who have the courage to defend it', was delivered by Flight Lieutenant G.E. Stirrup from the pulpit in the nave and the act of thanksgiving continued until, before the sounding of reveille and the return of the Colours to the bearers, the Chaplain-in-Chief of the Royal Air Force, the Venerable J.H. Wilson, CB, QHC, MA, read three verses from the Prophet Isaiah concluding with the exhortation: 'They that wait upon the Lord shall renew their strength: they shall mount up with wings as eagles; they shall run, and not be weary; and they shall walk, and not faint'. Bach's Fugue in G minor was played by the Central Band of the Royal Air Force and the Bells of the Abbey Church rung in a great peal as Her Majesty and their Royal Highnesses left.

The same year found another member of the Royal Family performing a very different public aviation duty, for on November 28, the Queen Mother drove to Hendon to carry out the opening ceremony of the Battle of Britain Museum and to unveil a plaque commemorating the ceremony. It was entirely appropriate for this royal lady had suffered a bomb on her London home at the height of the air fighting of the time.

Yet, while this triumphant opening was being carried out, triumphant because no public money had been involved in setting up the museum, Her Majesty the Queen was preparing for a trip by air that would take her half a world away while, at much the same time, other members of the Royal Family were in various parts of the globe with the aid of aircraft. On September 12 the Duke of Edinburgh had left Aberdeen's Dyce Airport in his capacity of President of the International Equestrian Federation to attend the World Three-Day Event Championships held in Lexington, Kentucky. 12 days later, Princess Margaret had flown from London Airport to Tuvalu and Dominica in order to represent the Queen at the independence celebrations there and at the beginning of the following month Prince Charles had been present at another celebration of the 60th anniversary of the Royal Air Force when he attended a dinner at the Headquarters of Strike Command at High Wycombe.

The new year of 1979 was that in which the new royal tour, already announced, was scheduled to take place and once more Heathrow was the starting point. The aircraft used to carry the Queen and the Duke of Edinburgh was a Concorde air liner and the fact no longer stimulated much emphasis in the news media, yet within the memories of many a trip in an early Comet was warranted attention. The destination was to be Riyadh Airport to visit the Saudi Arabian territories and also the trip was to include the United Arabian Emirates and Oman. However, this point on the schedule was not to be arrived at until February 17, five days after the departure from England, and, before this, the three-week tour was to cover Kuwait and Bahrain. But before this was history, Princess Alexandra, the

Honourable Mrs Angus Ogilvy, with her husband was to fly from London Airport as a representative of the Queen at the celebrations of independence on St Lucia, and it was to Heathrow that the Queen and the Duke of Edinburgh returned in Concorde on March 1. They would be back at London Airport in mid-May for a flying trip to Denmark for a State Visit.

A little earlier it had been announced from Buckingham Palace that Prince Andrew was to train as a Royal Navy helicopter pilot, thus becoming the third living member of the family to hold a 'chopper' certificate. The number of duties undertaken by the Royal Family all involving the use of aircraft is well shown by their itinerary for that year. Nor did the journeys all begin at home, as witness that made by Prince Charles in early April when he had flown from Canada to the Bahamas. However, it was the Duke of Kent who was to make a small piece of history in 1979 when he became the first member of the Royal Family to visit the Communist Republic of China where, in Peking, he was to open the British Energy Exhibition.

Botswana, Malawi, Tanzania and Zambia were scheduled to be visited during the summer of the same year and for this the Queen and the Duke of Edinburgh were joined by Prince Andrew who already had behind him some experience as a glider pilot when he had flown in a T21 glider from the RAF station at Milltown, with Flight Lieutenant Peter Bullivant as his instructor, during 1975. The return trip by the party was made from Lusaka on August 4.

Tragedy was to strike the Royal Family once more in the late summer of that year and aviation was to be involved, although this time only indirectly. On the afternoon of August 27 it was announced that Admiral of the Fleet Lord Mountbatten of Burma, had been killed by the blast of a bomb on board his boat *Shadow V* at Mullaghmore, County Sligo, and with him had died Nicholas Natchbull, his 14-year old grandson and, later in hospital, the Dowager Lady Brabourne from his immediate family. On August 30 the remains of these victims were flown from Ireland to Eastleigh in a Hercules of the RAF, XV223. The bearer party was found by personnel of the Queen's Flight and the first part of the journey in Ireland had been when the coffins were taken to the main airport in a pair of Sea King helicopters. The Duke of Edinburgh and Prince Charles were in England to meet the arrival and, in the case of Mountbatten, the nature of his homecoming was, although coincidental, entirely appropriate for a person who had used air transport so much during his service career and had even retained the York that had at one time belonged to Sir Keith Park.

Meanwhile the work of the Queen's Flight continued and towards the closure of the year it briefly sprang into public notice once more on the last day of the visit to Great Britain of Chairman Hua of the Peoples' Republic of China when, on November 4, a helicopter of the Flight was placed at his disposal.

The new decade of the 1980s found this unit still with not only the same type of equipment that it had been operating for ten years and more but also the actual machines, although there had been some agitation for the Flight to be furnished with fresh machines from several unofficial quarters for at least the preceding two years if not more. The arguments against this were chiefly based in an increasingly cost-conscious world on the demand for economy and, although such an attitude of mind is entirely praiseworthy and natural in a democracy, it fails to consider several important factors. Perhaps the most important of these ignores the lessons of history for, as we have seen in an earlier age when the aircraft operated by the British Royal Family has a nearer proximity to the prevailing ideas of modernity, the aircraft industry benefited in that countries abroad had more than sales endeavour to influence their final choice before orders were ultimately placed. They had seen with their own eyes concrete examples of reliability and standards of impeccable maintenance and there exists an unarguable fact that what a man has seen with his own eyes will have a much more salutary impact than that which is presented for his perusal by a vendor's paid servant, for the latter smacks too

Left *A royal Heron in use by the Queen Mother who is seen inspecting members of the Central Flying School Aerobatic Team.*

Right *Prince Andrew gliding at Milltown Airport, November 1975* (RAF News).

Right *Prince Andrew, later to train as a Naval helicopter pilot, familiarises himself with the controls of a glider.*

Right *XR486, in revised finish, hovers over XP299 which replaced XR487.*

much of an insult to his intelligence as it seems to indicate that he is expected to accept a pre-digested decision.

There is also the other psychological aspect with its political overtones that the Queen is a head of state and as such is a representative of a nation whose opinions, experience and influence is expected to be taken seriously in the world.

If an ordinary citizen goes to plead a cause, to state a case or enter upon any enterprise where he is expected to be taken seriously, unless he is entirely ignorant of the judgement of his fellows or the ways of the world, he approaches the undertaking by presenting his physical appearance in as good a light as possible. This analogy taken further to the equipment of the Queen's Flight finds Great Britain making a mistake not experienced by the United States, the Presidents of which nation arrive and depart from their journeys in sleek and modern jets capable, if not deliberately calculated, of giving an image in tune with its hoped-for world position. An example of just how strong is this factor may be found in a visit to America only a few years back when a Highland Regiment was scheduled to give a series of marching and musical displays. Sensible of their regimental pride and its history, the men that it featured spared no effort to present themselves in as near an approach to military perfection as was humanly possible and the impact on their audiences was electric. Military display on these lines had never been seen by the majority before and the enthusiasm of the regiment's reception was such that its members were being represented by the news media as the finest servicemen in the world! The psychological factor here worked in its most obvious form.

Another argument that has been encountered is that of the traditionalist and it is one that may be easily dismissed. The form it takes is that if the strength of a country's pride is placed on its past endeavour then the retention of somewhat elderly aircraft for the work of the Royal Flight, however near to perfection of serviceability they may be, is something on a par with, say, red tunics for the Brigade of Guards. It seems strange that adult human beings should seriously put forward

Above left *The cockpit of a Phantom is explained to Princess Anne when visiting RAF Bruggen to present the Queen's Colour to RAF Germany. On her right is Group Captain J.B. Curtiss* (Command Public Relations, RAF).
Left *Her Majesty the Queen alighting from XS790* (Crown Copyright).
Opposite page *Prince Charles at a conference at the RAF College, Cranwell, in February 1977 after promotion to Wing Commander. He was undergoing a week's refresher course to solo Jet Provost standard* (RAF News).

Air Commodore A.L. Winskill and the Duke of Edinburgh leave a Whirlwind helicopter at Benson (Crown Copyright).

something of this nature yet it has been done. This fails to recognise the difference between veteran and vintage and we would have had to advance to the point where, say, the 'maternity jacket' of the Royal Flying Corps has been invested by time with some sort of glamour before it was viable. Just possibly perhaps if the Queen's eldest son, when he ascends the throne, attends ceremonial functions by arriving in a Blériot monoplane, it could arguably be accepted, but then only in this country, for it takes hundreds of years before a glance and bow to the past of a nation becomes sufficiently remote to be accepted with a form of reverent tolerance abroad, and even this overlooks the psychological and political overtones already discussed.

There remains then, after several arguments that fail to look at the complete picture and at least one that is foolish, the question of costs. Here there are some surprises in store, for the latest available set of figures for the maintenance and running of the Queen's Flight is £2.4 million, a figure which does not take into consideration the re-sale value of the present aircraft which are capable of bringing back perhaps £1 million each on the United States market. For comparison, the annual maintenance costs for the Red Arrows aerobatic team over the same period is only a little lower at £2 million, while that for the maintenance of all the military bands in the United Kingdom has been stated to be £18 million.

Perhaps it was reasoned thinking along lines similar to these that prompted the announcement, early in 1980, that the Flight was likely to be re-equipped, at long last and with jet aircraft. Although at first this could not be confirmed from official sources, later this was remedied and it seemed likely that the BAC One-Eleven was the selected type although during the informal discussions with the British Aerospace industry the HS125, Jetstream and 146 were examined and discarded.

The actual model of the One-Eleven that had been selected was the Series 475, a machine with a span only three inches greater than the Andover but almost 16 feet longer, powered by two Rolls-Royce Spey-25 Mk 512DW turbofans, giving a range in excess of 1,500 miles at 550 mph. Advantages of the selected type include the fact that it is capable of using those airfields which had hitherto been unsuitable for jet passenger aircraft and had been restricted to propeller-driven air liners so that the scope of potential operations for the Queen's Flight would be in no way restricted by the graduation to pure jets. Additionally it is a type that, although entirely modern in concept, is based on a firm experience in that it combines the size of the fuselage associated with the earlier Series 400 with the engines of increased power from the Series 500 plus various aerodynamic improvements and a low pressure tyre system.

From this it will be seen that the selection of the type has been something of a compromise as must always be the case in the choice of aircraft for royal work, but the fact remains that the One-Eleven 475 was introduced in 1970 and the design may have to form the fixed-wing equipment of the Flight until perhaps 1995, a little before the entry into the new century—how will they compare with the air liners then current; has too conservative a choice been made?

The immediate factors governing the move appeared on February 18 1980 when the RAF Minister, Geoffrey Pattie, replied to a question in the House of Commons by the MP for Bexleyheath who had asked what financial arrangements had been made for the replacement of the Andovers. The question submitted that it should be fully realised that the present machines would have to be superseded and the cost of doing this would be proportionately higher the longer the change was left.

In his reply, Mr Pattie did not fail to point out that one reason for the long retention of the earlier machines was the ease with which they could be operated from small airfields, but any machine selected to take their place would have to be capable of much the same capability and also have an enhanced performance. He went on to refute the idea, rumoured in some quarters, that anything like a secret agreement had been made with the industry for the supply of two One-Elevens and emphasised that only general discussions had taken place which, at one time, even embraced the VC10, the only long-range VIP-machine then in use by the Royal Air Force.

Figures then revealed only proved what has been foreshadowed in this work, namely the enormous use of aircraft that is made by Her Majesty, so that any new machines with a range capable of taking them further than Western Europe would be welcome. It would, of course, be necessary for long range trips made by Her Majesty (for example, to Australia and New Zealand), to continue to use, as she presently does, aircraft either chartered from one of the major United Kingdom carriers, or an RAF (Australian Air Force, etc) VC10 or other long range aircraft. It was also made clear that the latest figures showed 35 per cent of all the flights undertaken by the Benson unit were made for the purpose of taking government ministers and Service chiefs about their business and the total number of journeys annually made is in the region of 700, 60 nations being visited in the space of five years. The question of re-equipment had been approved on two previous occasions by the Air Force Board, in 1972 and again in 1977 and although on both the BAC One-Eleven had been the type to be ordered, each time the proposal had been turned down. In an atmosphere of inflation and in the light of the arguments already stated this seems short sighted to say the least, particularly when viewed from the standpoint that, quite frequently, even emergent nations are alive to the importance of operating modern, jet-propelled aircraft for their heads of state.

All this must be regarded as part of the history of the Queen's Flight and to pretend otherwise is merely to take refuge in the comfortable safety of the past. The concept of its very existence was a bold and forward-looking idea in an age not yet completely orientated to navigation of the air, indeed only a little over 30 years after the pioneer trips of the Wright brothers; nearer in time in fact than we are to the first successful jet flight in Great Britain.

Today the Flight is part of No 38 Group, Air Support Command, by which it is controlled and consists of 140 officers and men with three fixed-wing aircraft and two helicopters in their charge. The Captain, unlike his two deputies, is a civilian and a member of the royal household. The work is decidedly in the unsocial hours bracket and quite frequently very long periods of time have to be put in one's particular field beyond the normal and so of air worthiness because there are no reserves in the way of back-up machines. Even so, to be appointed to the Flight in any capacity is a recognition of skill in one's particular field beyond the normal and so pilots, tradesmen and administrative staff extract a very real job satisfaction from what they are doing.

There are many reasons for this, perhaps one of them being that which was established in the days of Sir Edward Fielden's captaincy, namely a knowledge that one's superiors are sufficiently conversant with the work being done to recognise and appreciate skill when they see it. This applies beyond the

Queen Elizabeth, the Queen Mother, is welcomed to RAF Leeming by the Chief of Staff, Air Chief Marshal Sir Michael Beetham. Prince Andrew, who was currently serving with the Royal Naval Elementary Flying Training School, is in the background (RAF News).

In May 1980 Prince Andrew completed a 20-week fixed wing elementary flying training course at RAF Leeming. He is seen here with Squadron Leader Tony Harrison (left) and Flight Lieutenant David Walby (RAF News).

administrative structure of the Flight from the fact that two of the 'owners'—Prince Philip and Prince Charles—are experienced pilots of conventional aircraft and also helicopters. Soon this little group will be joined by Prince Andrew, who, like his elder brother, had also experienced parachuting, and who passed out as a 'chopper' pilot from the course which he began at HMS *Hermes* in February 1980. This began studies taking him via the Fleet Air Arm Safety and Survival School, Lee-on-Solent and RAF Leeming for ten months, to advanced training for a further 14 months at Culdrose Naval Air Station thus amassing flying hours far in excess of those of Her Majesty the Queen whose single helicopter experience, enforced by safety regulations, is confined to a flight to Northern Ireland in 1977.

Meanwhile it may well be that the Queen's Flight is about to embark on a new and exciting epoch in its existence, comparable with and perhaps exceeding that marked by the bold step towards modernisation taken in 1947. To oversee this, the Flight is well-blessed in the long-standing command and great experience of its Captain, Air Commodore Winskill, who has a dedication to his duties comparable to the remarkable standards set by his predecessors, qualities which were recognised at the end of the 1970s by the award of a popular and well-deserved knighthood.

How this navigation of the heavens by his decendants would have astonished King George III who, in 1784, turned from a window where he had been watching a balloon rise from Vauxhall Gardens and observed to his ministers '. . . we may never see poor Lunardi again'.

Appendices

1 Royal Air Force appointments in the Royal Family

Her Majesty the Queen
Air Commodore-in-Chief Royal Auxiliary Air Force; Air Commodore-in-Chief Royal Air Force Regiment; Air Commodore-in-Chief Royal Observer Corps; Honorary Air Commodore Royal Air Force, Marham; Commandant-in-Chief Royal Air Force College, Cranwell.

His Royal Highness the Prince Philip, Duke of Edinburgh, KG, KT, OM, GBE, PC
Marshal of the Royal Air Force; Marshal of the Royal Australian Air Force; Marshal of the Royal New Zealand Air Force; Air Commodore-in-Chief Air Training Corps; Honorary Air Commodore Royal Air Force, Kinloss.

Her Majesty Queen Elizabeth the Queen Mother
Commandant-in-Chief Women's Royal Air Force; Commandant-in-Chief Royal Air Force Central Flying School.

His Royal Highness the Prince of Wales, KG, KT, GCB
Wing Commander of the Royal Air Force; Air Commodore-in-Chief of the Royal New Zealand Air Force; Honorary Air Commodore Royal Air Force, Brawdy; Personal Aide-de-Camp to the Queen.

Her Royal Highness the Princess Anne, Mrs Mark Phillips, GCVO
Honorary Air Commodore Royal Air Force, Lyneham.

Her Royal Highness the Princess Margaret, Countess of Snowdon, CI, GCVO
Honorary Air Commodore Royal Air Force, Coningsby.

Her Royal Highness Princess Alexandra, the Honourable Mrs Angus Ogilvy, GCVO
Air Chief Commandant Princess Mary's Royal Air Force Nursing Service.

2 Captains of the Queen's Flight

1953-1962
Air Commodore Sir Edward H. Fielden, KCVO, CB, DFC, AFC (Formerly Captain of the King's Flight 1936-1941 and 1946-1953).
1962-1964
Air Commodore A.D. Mitchell, CVO, DFC and Bar, AFC
1964-1967
Air Commodore John H.L. Blount, DFC
Appointed 1968
Air Commodore Sir Archie L. Winskill, KCVO, CBE, DFC and Bar, AE, MRAeS.

3 The North African Flight, 1943: Aircraft, Crew and Passengers

Avro York LV633 Ascalon
Pilot Wing Commander H.B. Collins, DFC; *Second Pilot* Flight Lieutenant E.G. Fraser; *Navigational Officer* Squadron Leader J.L. Mitchell, DFC; *Signals Officer* Flight Lieutenant W. Gallagher; *Flight Engineer* Flight Lieutenant S.S. Payne, DFM; *Relief Pilot* Wing Commander C.E. Slee, AFC; *Additional Engineer* Flight Lieutenant T. Jenkins; *CATCO, Transport Command Headquarters* Wing Commander J. Jeffs; *Steward* Corporal H. Sheppard.
Passengers, Outward Journey
His Majesty King George VI; *Private Secretary* Major the Right Honourable Sir Alexander Hardinge, GCVO, KCB, MC; *Master of the Royal Household* Colonel the Honourable Sir Piers Legh, KCVO,

CMG, CIE, OBE; *Air Equerry* Group Captain Edward H. Fielden, MVO, AFC; *Deputy C-in-C, North Africa* General the Honourable Sir Harold Alexander, GCB, CSI, DSO, MC; *Secretary of State for Air* Sir Archibald Sinclair, Bt, KT, CMG, MP; *Royal Army Medical Corps Officer* Lieutenant-Colonel Richardson; *GSOI* Lieutenant-Colonel Gault; *Metropolitan Police Officers* Staff Sergeants H. Cameron, R.J. Evitts and T.L. Jerrons.

Passengers, Homeward Journey
The passenger list for this flight was exactly as on the outward journey except that it did not include General Alexander, his place being occupied by: *Crown Equerry* Colonel D. McM. Kavanagh, CVO.

3a Crew of General Sir Henry Maitland Wilson's Dakota, 1944

(Aircraft *Freedom* used by King George VI in Italy). Squadron Leader P.E. Penfold (Pilot); Flight Lieutenant E.K. Burton; Flight Lieutenant S.E. Callaghan; Flight Lieutenant J.C.G. Osborn.

4 The King's Flight, 1946: Aircraft, Crews and Staff

King's Aircraft-Viking VL246
Pilot Wing Commander E.W. Tacon, DSO, DFC, AFC; *Second Pilot* Flight Lieutenant A.J. Lee; *Navigational Officer* Flight Lieutenant D. Fowkes; *Signals Officer* Flight Lieutenant L.G.S. Reed, DFC.

Queen's Aircraft-Viking VL247
Pilot Squadron Leader H.F. Payne, AFC; *Second Pilot* Flight Lieutenant P.G. Tilbrook; *Navigational Officer* Flight Lieutenant A. Knapper, AFC; *Signals Officer* Flight Lieutenant D.J. Dartmouth.

Staff Aircraft-Viking VL245
Pilot Flight Lieutenant W.E. Welch; *Second Pilot* Flight Lieutenant A.E. Richmond; *Navigational Officer* Flight Lieutenant A.P. O'Hara, DFC, DFM; *Signals Officer* Flight Lieutenant P.H. McKenna, DFM.

Workshop Aircraft-Viking VL248
Pilot Flight Lieutenant R.J. Harrison; *Second Pilot* Flight Lieutenant E.B. Trubshaw; *Navigational Officer* Flight Lieutenant W.E. Boteler, DFC; *Signals Officer* Flight Lieutenant F. Myers, AFC; *Staff Adjutant* Flight Lieutenant L.T. Reid; *Chief Flight Engineering Officer* Flight Lieutenant A.A. Morley, DFC, DFM; *Ground Engineering Officer* Flight Lieutenant G.A. Pearson; *Equipment and Accounts Officer* Squadron Leader H. Wright; *Engineer Fitter* Corporal N.W.P. Southall; *Airframe Fitter* Leading Aircraftsman N.E. Thorn; *Engine Fitters* Aircraftsmen (First Class) G.F. Edginton and A. Edwards; *Maintenance Assistant* Aircraftsman (Second Class) P. Ferguson; *Radio Mechanic* Sergeant W.T. Clapperton; *Electrician* Sergeant T.E. Shore; *Instrument Repairer* Corporal D.A. Sealey; *Aircraft Finisher* Sergeant E. Ward; *Safety Equipment* Corporal W.J. Brownlee; *Steward* Sergeant W.P. Jack.

5 The King's Flight, 1948: Aircraft, Crews and Staff

King's Aircraft-Viking VL246
Pilot Wing Commander E.W. Tacon, DSO, DFC, AFC; *Second Pilot* Squadron Leader H.A. Nash, AFC; *Navigational Officer* Flight Lieutenant D. Fokes; *Signals Officer* Flight Lieutenant L.G.A. Reed, MVO, DFC; *Flight Engineer* Flight Lieutenant K.C. Hampson, DFC.

Queen's Aircraft-Viking VL247
Pilot Squadron Leader H.F. Payne, MVO, AFC; *Navigational Officer* Flight Lieutenant A. Browne; *Signals Officer* Flight Lieutenant F. Myers, AFM; *Flight Engineer* Flight Lieutenant J.F.W. Yates, DFC.

Staff Aircraft One-Viking, VL232
Pilot Flight Lieutenant A.J. Lee; *Navigational Officer* Flight Lieutenant J. Higgins; *Signals Officer* Flight Lieutenant K. Gamble; *Flight Engineer* Flight Lieutenant H.J. Redding.

Staff Aircraft Two-Viking VL233
Pilot Flight Lieutenant S.N. Sloan, DFC, GCM; *Navigational Officer* Flight Lieutenant M.E.H. Dawson, DFC, DFM; *Signals Officer* Flight Lieutenant M.P. Davies; *Flight Engineer* Flight Lieutenant L.D. Pope, DFC.

Workshop Aircraft-Viking VL248
Pilot Flight Lieutenant E.B. Trubshaw; *Navigational Officer* Flight Lieutenant E. Brewin; *Signals Officer* Flight Lieutenant P.H. McKenna, DFM; *Flight Engineer* Flight Lieutenant E. Yates; *Staff Adjutant* Flight Lieutenant D.J. Rogers; *Flight Engineering Officers* Squadron Leader G.A. Pearson, MVO and Flight Lieutenant T. Bussey, BEM; *Equipment and Secretarial Officer* Flight Lieutenant L.W. Denning.

6 Royal visit to Australia, 1970: Aircraft, Crews and Staff

BAC One-Eleven A12-125
Pilot Wing Commander R.F. Drury, AFC; *Second*

Pilot Flight Lieutenant J.D. Grierson; *Navigational Officer* Squadron Leader N. Reidy; *Flight Engineer* Corporal R.T. Tarrant; *Stewardess* Corporal J. Grant; *Stewards* Sergeant D. Brumfield and Corporal D. Donnelly.

Hawker Siddeley HS-748

Pilot Flight Lieutenant F. Adams; *Second Pilot* Squadron Leader A. Matters; *Navigational Officer* Flight Lieutenant S. Cattell.

6a Flights during royal tour of Australia

6-7 April Melbourne-Swan Hill-Portland-Melbourne (Victoria).
10 April Wellangong-RAAF Williamtown (NSW).
28 April Canberra-Armidale (NSW)-Sydney.
29 April Orange (NSW)-RAAF Richmond (NSW).

7 Official Royal Aircraft, 1936-1974

Type	Identity	Used	Date	Remarks
de Havilland DH89A Rapide	G-ADDD	Edward VIII	1936	King's personal property
Airspeed AS6 Envoy III	G-AEXX	George VI	1937	Air Ministry property
Lockheed L-214 Hudson	N7263, N7364		1939	Only armed royal aircraft
Percival Q6 Petrel	P5634		1940	Became G-AHTB
de Havilland DH 95 Flamingo	G-AGCC		1940	Little used
King's Flight disbanded February 14 1941				
Avro 685 York	LV633	George VI and Prime Minister	1943/4	*Ascalon*
Douglas DC-3 Dakota III & IV	KG770, KN386	Both King and Queen	1945	
King's Flight reformed May 1 1946				
Vickers VC1 Viking C2	VL245	Staff aircraft		Delivered 1947
	VL246	George VI		Delivered 1947
	VL247	Queen Elizabeth		Delivered 1947
	VL248	Workshop aircraft		Delivered Aug 1946
	VL232	Replacement of VL245		Delivered July 1948
	VL233	Australian Tour		Delivered July 1948
Westland-Sikorsky R-4B	KL106	Carriage of mail	1947	Delivered Aug 8
Hoverfly I	KL110	between Dyce and	1947	Delivered Aug 6
	KK973	Balmoral	1947	Delivered Aug 25
	KL104	As above, all from RN	1948	Delivered July 29
	KK987		1948	Delivered July 10
Unit renamed Queen's Flight				
de Havilland DHC1 Chipmunk	VP861, WP903	Duke of Edinburgh	1952	Delivered Nov, to store Aug 1964
de Havilland DH104 Devon	VP961	Duke of Edinburgh	1953	On loan to Queen's Flight
Westland HC4 Dragonfly	XF261		1954	
de Havilland DH114 Heron	XH375	Duke of Edinburgh	1955	Delivered May
	XM295, XM296	Viking replacement	1958	Delivered April 11, XM296 later to RN
Westland Whirlwind HAR 4	XL111	Dragonfly replacement	1958	
Westland Whirlwind HCC8	XN126, XN127		1958	
Douglas DC-3 Dakota IV	KN452, KN645	Queen's Asian Tour	1961	
de Havilland DH114 Heron C4	XR391		1961	Delivered June, later to RN
Westland Whirlwind HCC12	XR486, XR487	Replacement of XN126/127	1964	Delivered June, XR487 lost 1967
Hawker-Siddeley HS-748 Andover	XS789	Replaced XH375	1964	Delivered July
	XS790	Replaced XM295	1964	Delivered Aug
	XS793	Replaced XM296	1968	

Westland Whirlwind HAR10	XP299	Replaced XR487	1968	Delivered on loan February
de Havilland DHC1 Chipmunk	WP912	Prince Charles' solo	1968	Trained on WP903
Westland Wessex HCC4	XV732	Replaced XR486	1968	Delivered June 25
	XV733	Replaced XP299	1968	Delivered June 30
Vickers VC10	XV107	For visit to S. America	1968	
Beagle B206Z Basset CC1	XS770	For Prince of Wales	1969	
Westland Wessex HCC4	XV726	Replaced XV732	1969	Flotation gear,
	XV727	Replaced XV733	1969	modified noses
BAC One-Eleven	A12-125	On Australian Tour	1970	From 34 Sqdn RAAF, April
Hawker Siddeley HS-748	A10-596	On Australian Tour	1970	From 34 Sqdn RAAF
Westland Wessex 5	XT481	Led Yeovilton Wessex flypast	1974	Flown by Prince Charles

8 Aircraft officially associated with Edward, Prince of Wales, 1928-1935

Type	Identity	Date	Remarks
Bristol F2B	J8430	1928	No 24 Squadron
Westland Wapiti Mk IA	J9095	1928	Delivered June 26
	J9096		Delivered June 27
de Havilland DH 60M Gipsy Moth	G-AALG	1929	
Hawker Tomtit	J9772	1930	No 24 Squadron
Hawker Tomtit	G-AALL		King's Cup entrant
de Havilland DH 60M Gipsy Moth	G-ABCW	1930	Later damaged June 18
de Havilland DH 60X Gipsy Moth	G-ABDB	1930	Replaced G-ABCW
de Havilland DH 80 Puss Moth	G-ABBS	1930	Dual controls
Fairey IIIF	J9061	1930	No 24 Squadron
	K1115		No 24 Squadron
de Havilland DH 80 Puss Moth	G-ABNN	1931	Replaced 'BBS
Westland Wessex	G-ABEG	1931	
de Havilland DH 83 Fox Moth	G-ACDD	1932	To Belgium as OO-ENC, then Egypt 1933, Congo 1934 and Air Travel New Zealand as ZK-AEK, 1935
Vickers 259 Viastra MkX	G-ACCC	1932	
de Havilland DH 84 Dragon	G-ACGG	1933	
de Havilland DH 89 Dragon Rapide	G-ADDD		
	G-ACTT	1935	

9 King's Cup Winners, 1922-1980

Pilot	Type	Identity	Speed (mph)	Year
F.L. Barnard	DH4A	G-EAMU	124	1922
F.T. Courtney	A.W. Siskin II	G-EBEU	149	1923
A.J. Cobham	DH50	G-EBFN	107	1924
F.L. Barnard	A.W. Siskin V	G-EBLQ	142	1925
H.S. Broad	DH60 Moth	G-EBMO	90	1926
W.L. Hope	DH60 Moth	G-EBME	91	1927
W.L. Hope	DH60G Gipsy Moth	G-EBYZ	106	1928
F/O R. Atcherly	Gloster Grebe II	J7520	150	1929
Miss W.S. Brown	Avro Avian III	G-EBVZ	103	1930
F/O E. Edwards	Blackburn Bluebird	G-AACC	118	1931
W.L. Hope	DH83 Fox Moth	G-ABUT	124	1932
G. de Havilland	DH85 Leopard Moth	G-ACHD	140	1933
F/Lt H. Schofield	Monospar ST-10	G-ACTS	134	1934

F/Lt T. Rose	Miles Falcon Six	G-ADLC	176	1935
C.E. Gardner	Percival Vega Gull	G-AEKE	164	1936
C.E. Gardner	Percival Mew Gull	G-AEKL	234	1937
A. Henshaw	Percival Mew Gull	G-AEXF	236	1938
J.N. Somers	Miles M65 Gemini	G-AKDC	164	1949
E. Day	Miles M14 Hawk	G-AKRV	139	1950
G. Gregory	Taylorcraft D	G-AHGZ	114	1952
W. Fillingham	DHC1 Chipmunk	G-AKDN	142	1953
F/Lt H. Wood	Miles M28 Messenger	G-AKBO	133	1954
P. Clifford	Percival Mew Gull	G-AEXF	214	1955
J.H. Denyer	Auster J-1	G-AJRH	124	1956
F. Dunkerley	Miles M77 Sparrowjet	G-ADNL	228	1957
J.H. Denyer	DH82A Tiger Moth	G-AIVW	119	1958
A.J. Spiller	Percival Proctor	G-AHFK	143	1959
S/L J. Severne	Rollason Turbulent*	G-APNZ	109	1960
S/L H.B. Iles	Miles M18	G-AHKY	142	1961
P.S. Clifford	Tipsy Nipper 2	G-ARDY	101	1962
P. Bannister	Tipsy Nipper 2	G-APYB	103	1963
D.M. Hartas	LeVier Cosmic Wind	G-ARUL	185	1964
J. Stewart-Wood	Cessna 172B	G-ARYS	132	1965
J.A. Miles	DHC1 Chipmunk	G-APTS	135	1966
C. Masefield	NA P-51D Mustang	N6356T	278	1967
S/L F.R. Hayter	DH87 Hornet Moth	G-ADKM	121	1968
R. d'Erlanger	Rollason Turbulent	G-ASAM	100	1969
M.A. Pruden	Champion Citabria	N7566F	130	1970
J.A. Bradshaw	Percival Provost I	G-AWPH	205	1971
S.A. Warwick	Airtourer Super 150	G-AZBE	165	1972
H.W. Bonner	DHC1 Chipmunk	G-ARWB	143	1973
J. Behrman	Piper Comanche	G-ARSK	187	1974
J. Cull	Bolkow Junior	G-ATYP	129	1975
A.J. Spiller	Cessna 180	G-ASIT	163	1976
A. Chadwick	Rollason Beta	G-AWHZ	197	1977
J. Stewart-Wood	Seneca Racer	G-BDRI	200	1978
Dr. I. Dalziel	Miles Falcon	G-AEEG	136	1979
A.J. Spiller	Cessna 180	G-ASIT	162	1980

* The entrant was the Duke of Edinburgh, the pilot, his equerry. This was the first time that the King's Cup has been won by a royal entry.

10 Representative use of Royal Aircraft, 1955-1968

Aircraft Type and Period of Use

de Havilland Heron Mk III: XM375, May 1955-September 1964.

de Havilland Heron Mk IV: XM295, April 1958-January 1965; XM296, April 1958-July 1968; XM391, June 1961-June 1968.

Major Tours Undertaken

1958 (November) Ethiopia, British Somaliland and Aden by The Duke and Duchess of Gloucester.

1959 (February) Kenya and Uganda by The Queen Mother; (March) Africa, the Middle East and Mediterranean area by Major General Moore; (April) Nigeria by The Duke and Duchess of Gloucester; (November) West Africa by HRH Prince Philip.

1960 (March) Africa by the GOC London District; (May) Rhodesia and Nyasaland by The Queen Mother; (September) Nigeria by Princess Alexandra.

1961 (January) India and Pakistan by HM The Queen and HRH Prince Philip; (February) Nepal by HM The Queen and HRH Prince Philip; (April) Sierra Leone by The Duke of Kent; (November) Burma, Thailand and the Far East by Princess Alexandra; (November) Ghana, Sierra Leone, Gambia and Tanganyika by HM The Queen and HRH Prince Philip.

1962 (February) Africa by The Duke and

Duchess of Gloucester; (May) Canada and the United States by HRH Prince Philip; (November) Uganda, Tanzania and Kenya by The Duke and Duchess of Kent.

1963 (March) Jordan and the Near East by The Duke and Duchess of Gloucester.

Representative passengers

HM The Queen
HRH Prince Philip, Duke of Edinburgh
HM The Queen Mother
HRH Princess Margaret, Countess of Snowdon
HRH Prince Charles
TRH The Duke and Duchess of Gloucester
HRH The Princess Royal
TRH The Duke and Duchess of Kent
HRH Princess Marina
TRH Prince William and Prince Richard of Gloucester
HRH Prince Michael of Kent
HRH Princess Alice, Countess of Athlone
HG The Duke of Norfolk
HM The King of Norway
TM The King and Queen of Thailand
HM King Hussein of Jordan
HRH Princess Aida of Ethiopia
HRH Princess Muna
HRH The Princess of Chandhaburi
HRH Prince Carl Gustav of Sweden
Lord Hailsham
Lord Jellico
Dr Nkrumah
General Mobutu
Sir Alec Douglas Home
HE The President of Finland
HE The President of Senegal
HE The President of India
Right Honourable R.A. Butler
Right Honourable Harold Macmillan
Right Honourable Edward Heath
Right Honourable Harold Wilson
Mr Robert Kennedy
Mr Robert Mac Namara
Mr Cyrus Vance
Mr Pandit Nehru

Total number of flights carried out: 941
Total distance flown: 2,000,000 miles
Total flying time: 13,400 hours

NB Titles and descriptions of persons and place names are those in use during the period described.

Selected Bibliography

Birch, Neville and Branson, Alan, *Captains and Kings* (Pitman, 1972).

Butcher, Percy E, *Skill and Devotion* (Radio and Control Press, 1971).

Courtney, Frank T., *Flight Path* (Kimber, 1972).

Donaldson, Frances, *Edward VIII* (Weidenfeld & Nicolson, 1974).

Garnier, Peter, *Royal Wings, an Anthology* (IPC Transport Press, 1977).

Hering, S/L Peter G., *Customs and Traditions of the Royal Air Force* (Gale and Polden, 1961).

Judd, Dennis, *The Life and Times of George V* (Weidenfeld & Nicolson, 1973).

Learmouth, Bob and Nash, Miss Joanna, *The First Croydon Airport* (Sutton Libraries & Art Services, 1977).

Lewis, Peter, *British Racing and Record Breaking Aircraft* (Putnam, 1970).

McCudden, James B., *Five Years in the Royal Flying Corps* (John Hamilton, 1918, republished, 1930).

Middlemas, Keith, *George VI* (Weidenfeld & Nicolson, 1974).

Moyes, Philip J.R., (Ed), *Aircraft Annual 1977* (Ian Allan, 1976).

Nicolson, Sir Harold, *King George V, His Life and Reign* (Constable, 1970).

Robertson, Bruce, *British Military Aircraft Serials* (Patrick Stephens, 1979).

Robertson, Bruce, *The RAF, a Pictorial History* (Robert Hale, 1978).

Rochford, Leonard H., *I Chose the Sky* (Kimber, 1977).

Vincent, Air Vice-Marshal Stanley, *Flying Fever* (Jarrolds, 1972).

Wheeler-Bennet, Sir John, *King George VI, His Life and Reign* (Macmillan, 1958).

Index